𝕱𝖆𝖒
𝖂𝖔𝖒𝖊𝖓 𝖎𝖓 𝕯𝖔𝖗𝖘𝖊𝖙

Elizabeth Edwards

Power Publications

© Power Publications
1 Clayford Avenue
Ferndown
Dorset BH22 9PQ

ISBN 0-9514-502-9-8

Publishers Note
Whilst every care has been taken to ensure the accuracy of
all the facts and information in this book neither the
author nor the publisher or printers can accept
responsibility for any inaccuracies.

Front cover painting: by Emily Goddard

Printed by Cathedral Print Services Ltd, Rollestone Street, Salisbury SP1 1DX

ACKNOWLEDGEMENTS

I would like to express my gratitude to the following who have helped me in many ways and have expressed their belief that a book making women the central characters will indicate that in all periods women have had an important role in the progress of the country.

Margaret Brown, MBE
George Bruce
Peggy Butcher
Edna Dawes
Harry Edwards
Leigh Hatts

Pamela Hamilton Howard
  of Langtry Manor Hotel
Karen London
Dr. Ted Ward
Mrs. Yorke Batley

Photographs, or permission to rephotograph have been kindly provided by the following:

Sylvia Bowditch
Harry Edwards
Fabian Society
Doreen Forshaw

Karen London
The National Trust
Poole Museums
Suzanne Sieger

INDEX

Corfe Castle in 1643

LADY MARY BANKES
The Courageous Defender of Corfe Castle

Though gaunt and ruined, Corfe Castle still stands with pride towering above the little village of Corfe and the surrounding countryside. The castle, which was once a royal demesne and the residence of the rich and powerful, still attracts thousands of people each year who come to admire and wonder at its past history. The castle dated back to the time of King Alfred and other royal personages, while in March, A.D. 978 a dastardly crime was committed by Queen Elfrida, the second wife of King Edgar, who callously effected the murder of her stepson, King Edward, by stabbing him in the back.

By purchase, in 1634, Corfe Castle came into the possession of Sir John Bankes, an eminent lawyer, a Chief Justice, and a devoted follower of King Charles I. His wife, Mary, was the daughter of the ancient family of HAWTREYS of Ruislip, Middlesex. The castle, with its thick walls and elevated commanding position, was considered impregnable. Even so, Sir John and his men, all ardent supporters of the King's cause, felt anxious about leaving their wives and families un-protected, except for a small garrison of five soldiers and a few faithful retainers – as they left with sadness in their hearts, to join the King's standard at Oxford.

5

Despite the fighting between Cromwell and the Roundheads against King Charles and his Cavalier followers, life in the castle continued quite normally. The children spent pleasant days in the nearby country, while Lady Bankes, or Dame Mary, as she was affectionately known, was often occupied making household wines and conserves. There was also embroidery, tapestry work and even spinning to provide the household linen.

Lady Bankes, although no longer young, still had a fair and unwrinkled face, with attractive brown ringlets curling over her forehead. Her voice was pleasant and the children loved to listen to her many tales of the past. Until May 1643 the occupants of the castle were left in peace. May 1st was always a time of excitement and festivity. That day Dame Mary prepared a great banquet for her retainers, which was followed by a stag hunt the next day, a custom which dated back to ancient days.

But in the castle was a false retainer, a malcontent named Simon Sturge, had secretly agreed to lead a party of Roundheads by an unknown lane to the postern gate, usually left unfastened for the return of the hunters, and where the enemy troops might be able to enter the castle. From the Tower Lady Bankes and her children saw, to their dismay, horsemen making their way to the castle. Quickly she raced to the postern gate, locking it firmly against suspected invaders. Fortunately her huntsmen and followers arrived first, calling out, "We are betrayed; Cromwell's men are upon us." "What shall we do?" but without a moment's hesitation the brave lady said with pride and determination, "We will defend ourselves."

From the Keep they could watch the attacking party, who quickly realised that they had no chance of entering by the postern gate. When the invaders saw the cannons which had been arranged along the ramparts, they accused Lady Bankes of bringing ammunition within the fortress. Parliamentary authorities in the neighbourhood demanded that she deliver the guns immediately. This, she refused to do, but agreed to dismount them, and for a few days the Roundheads left the castle in peace.

Fear spread among the occupants of the castle, as rumours circulated that another attack would shortly be made, If they were besieged for a long time there would be the problem of adequate provisions. There were, however, sheep and cows on the nearby slopes if they were able to get near them.

After the midday meal, Lady Bankes addressed her household and garrison and asked quietly if they would be willing to aid her in protecting the castle. Agreement was unanimous; everyone was then given a task, to look to the guns, guard the provisions and watch continually from the tower. Bravely, she exclaimed, "May God help the right and be to us a strong tower in the face of our enemies." Preparations for remounting the guns on their carriages at a moment's warning, were carefully made. Ammunition was carried to points where it would be most ready for action. Although Dame Mary remained calm, her retainers could sense the anxiety in her heart. Women were collecting the provisions and examining barrels of saltmeat, and flour. The cook was busily occupied preparing food for a siege by making large pies and boiling rounds of beef. When doubt crept in among some of her followers, Dame Mary advised them to lie down and rest. "You have earned it well and will need all your strength to-morrow. "I know you are my good friends and soldiers."

Shortly afterwards they were threatened by a group of sailors demanding surrender of the cannons. Courteously Lady Bankes asked to know by whose authority she was requested to surrender them. Their warrant from Parliament was produced and they demanded that the gates be opened to them. Her reply was that at the desire of the Commissioners the guns had been taken off their carriages and a promise given that if they were dismounted she would not be disturbed by their possession. But the men insisted that they had received orders to take away the guns and again demanded that the gates be opened to them. But the answer came a few moments afterwards with the thunder of a report from the ramparts frightening the 'brave' mariners so much that they ran away as fast as they could. Retaliation was swift as the enemy adopted more stringent methods of preventing food from getting to them by forbidding those in the neighbourhood from supplying any food to the castle, on pain of punishment.

Lady Bankes, who was sure of the goodwill of the men of the island and of the tenants and retainers of her husband, summoned her friends to come to her assistance, by beating a drum. Soon a large party arrived bringing with them a supply of firearms. But the castle was under continuous watch and when a young lad attempted to surreptiously bring gunpowder to the castle, he was stopped and his goods confiscated.

Warning letters were received from the Roundheads assuring Lady Bankes that no harm would befall her but she *must* surrender the cannons which had already been used against their envoys, and then she would be molested no further.

There were more problems, when the castle was approached by a crowd of anxious women who had also received threatening letters informing them that their homes could be burnt and destroyed if assistance was given to the castle. They begged that their husbands be allowed to return with them to protect them from the awful danger of their cottages being destroyed. The kind dame realised their concern and immediately sent their menfolk back to their homes. To appease her enemies, Lady Bankes agreed to allow them to have her guns, with the result that the Roundheads reduced the watch on the castle.

Unexpected help came from Captain Bond, an old Cavalier, who, with 20 soldiers offered their help in defending the castle. With the previous garrison of five men and some Loyalists who came to assist, their little army had grown to 40 fighting men. The growing number of supporters meant more worries about the lessening quantity of food.

To their dismay, the enemy then increased its number to 600 men, who gathered, watched and waited on the hillsides, like vultures ready for their prey, knowing that the castle was practically in their hands. They felt sure there could be little trouble when they decided to storm it.

Sir John was at that time proceeding to Salisbury for the summer circuit of assizes, where he had caused further anger from the Roundheads by denouncing the Earl of Essex and others who had combined in arms against the King. Although an urgent message had been sent to Sir John there was no reply, and the fears of Lady Bankes mounted. The younger members of the family still fed the poultry with grain and saw that they had adequate drinking water, including the ducks and one magnificent peacock. Noticing the pigeons flying about, son Ralph decided to send a message by carrier pigeon, an idea agreed by his mother, even though the birds had only been partially trained.

Two were sent off in case the first one did not get through. Food was getting scarcer all the time and there was real fear of famine within the castle walls. The enemy still waited outside. With sadness in their hearts, the peacock was eaten, followed by hens and ducks, but the castle was still standing in its dignity and strength. Threats and demands for surrender were made from time to time, followed by cannon shots, the enemy hoping that, as a result, a flag of truce would be flown with a request for terms. The air of incertitude continued until June 1643. From that time, hostilities really began and continued almost unceasingly until the middle of August.

Lady Bankes made her usual rounds, while her daughter, Dorothy, and niece Evelyn, embroidered in the Queen's Tower with wide windows, which looked upon the gardens below. Although the room was cold they dare not light a fire owing to the shortage of coal and wood. To protect the silver goblets, containers and other precious items from theft, they were lowered into one of the wells. That particular night as they admired the twinkling stars, Ralph noticed the movement of men and bright lights, the enemy was preparing to attack. At break of day the attack began in deadly earnest and continued throughout the day, while the 40 soldiers in the castle, showed their bravery and skill as they defended the castle against the undisciplined forces of the Roundheads.

The Waiting maids refreshed the soldiers with flagons of wine and bowls of soup. At the end of the day the besiegers left for shelter in the village, and quietness reigned for a time. Weary soldiers unlaced their corslets and lay down wearily on the floor while Lady Bankes dressed the wounds of a few of her men who had been hurt. The tired men were given food and tried to rest before the next attack. Everyone was worn out and the members of the household took to their beds in readiness for the morning. Fortunately the strong walls of the castle had scarcely been touched by the many cannon shots.

Shortly afterwards, the two girls, Mary and Evelyn, watched anxiously from their place in the keep at the curious proceedings in the village. Men were placing ladders to the church, climbing on the roof and stripping off the lead to make more bullets.

Simon Sturge, the deceitful traitor, suddenly returned to the castle, full of remorse for his acts, and gratitude for Dame Mary's care of his wife and children who had all been ill. He brought important news about the enemy, who had broken up the organ in the church, melted some of the pipes; others were used to hold their powder, and the men had even cut up surplices for shirts for themselves. Simon described them as a poor type of soldier with no confidence in their leader, Sir Walter Erle, and who often argued and fought among themselves. They had been bribed to storm the castle again with promises of a share in the rich spoils expected from the castle, silver, jewels and gold pieces, and would show no mercy to the occupants.

Lack of food was an ever increasing problem, and Simon, to show his gratefulness, volunteered to drive in some of the oxen from the hills near Wareham, aided by his eldest son.

More days of quietness follows, then suddenly, there was another attack and the thunder of the culverins was heard again.

Life in the castle was hectic, with Dame Mary and others casting bullets, some were rolling up mattresses and bedding on which they had been lying. Lady Bankes insisted that the men take refreshments before their work began, for she felt that this was to be a most violent attack. Rumours had been circulated that there were traitors in the castle itself, and that half of the party were secretly on the side of the Commonwealth. This was stoutly denied by the brave lady. "I certainly do not believe this" she averred. "You have all done me good service and I know you will do it again. My husband, who is Lord Chief Justice will reward you well for your efforts – and our walls are strong." A cheer filled the hall, while all knelt as Lady Bankes read a few short supplications from the Book of Common Prayer. This was followed by great bowls of porridge.

The siege was on again. The enemy had provided themselves with scaling ladders and were well primed with strong drink. Wooden structures had been formed to enable the men to breach the castle under safe cover.

Unfortunately for them, their legs were visible and castle marksmen could aim effectively. The scaling ladders were next brought forward, while her supporters used firing rams and spears. Lady Bankes and her valiant women, despite their horror of fighting and bloodshed, rained hot cinders and stones to prevent the attackers from scaling the walls. In between she managed to give words of encouragement to her own men. When the enemy finally withdrew, about 100 of their men had been wounded or killed.

Deeply worried at no news from Sir John and also the reduced quantity of food, their close confinement was beginning to tell on the nerves of the occupants of the castle, and gloomy thoughts were often in their minds.

A sleepless night was followed by the dawn and active work of preparing for another assault. Coals were heaped in the huge chimneys so that supplies of hot embers would be ready to throw on besieging attackers. Despite her fears and worries, Lady Bankes called her household for prayers to the one above who was a refuge to those who trusted in him.

The assault commenced with more fury than before. The enemy and their leader, Sir Walter Erle, were becoming more enraged by the long resistance. Scaling ladders were brought to the steepest part of the walls and men mounted with wild fire in their hands, ready to be thrown down into the castle, but as they mounted they were repulsed by the fire of small arms or spears from the soldiers on the walls. Lady Mary and her women rained hot embers on the enemy, while other women prepared food and wine for the men and tended the wounded.

Suddenly the fog came and the hills could no longer be seen under a thick, impenetrable blanket, with the further threat of an unobserved entrance by the enemy. A reward of £20 had been offered to the first man to scale the walls, and smaller amounts to those who followed. All the opposers seemed to be plentiful supplied with spirits. Careful watch had to be maintained throughout the day in all parts of the castle, with the fog becoming ever thicker. The strain and anxiety was great. Lady Bankes would not leave her post even to eat, but her devoted daughter and her niece brought her a basin of hot soup, persuaded her to eat while they took over sentinel duty. Eventually they realised that most of the soldiers outside the walls had retreated, and as the fog lifted, they could see parties carrying away dead and wounded. Darkness came and then another dawn, and with it little hope of maintaining their position. But relief was at hand. A secret message arrived with the news that the King's forces were advancing, and also a letter from Sir John who had been on circuit in Cambridge and who had only recently heard of the perils of the family. He was on his way to join them as quickly as possible and he begged them to be of good cheer.

The journey to Corfe was difficult, with atrocious roads, thick with mud and deep ruts, and several times the forces lost their way. Coaches stuck fast in the slime and mud, but Sir John, anxious to be home, decided to travel ahead on horseback with one of his attendants. He was conscious of the perils, not only from absent soldiers, but also from highwaymen who infested the thick forests and the lonely waste lands.

The prisoners in the castle were pale with watching. Hope had been crushed, until the letter came from Sir John, when their spirits became brighter once more. Lady Bankes, quite exhausted, rested in the solitude of her room. The Roundheads had evidently heard of the approaching troops as all remained quiet outside. To the delight of all, a horseman was seen approaching – it was – it was – Sir John. There was joy and thanksgiving all around. An army, headed by Prince Rupert, was on its way to protect the inmates of the castle and which had also met with Sir John at a certain stage. As they neared Wareham, they heard many reports of the ferocious attacks on the castle.

When all the greetings were over, Sir John praised his wife for her wonderful efforts in protecting the castle. "Well and bravely have you kept the Roundheads at bay. All the court is ringing with your praises, dear Dame Mary. I wish you could hear the handsome remarks of the King and Queen about you."

Soon they were welcoming the Royalist leaders who had been waiting outside the castle. They, too, were full of praise for Lady Bankes and the gallant way the enemy had been repulsed, but there was some damage. The small towers, along with the outer walls, had been practically destroyed. Even the strong outer wall had been considerably battered. The gate beyond the four-arched bridge was a wreck of stones and mortar, but the castle itself was barely scarred, still looking as strong and stately as previously.

Congratulations were given by the knights to Sir John, who then presented them to his wife, his daughter, Dorothy and his niece, Evelyn. From being tired and heavy-eyed the ladies had become bright with joy, and had all made a special effort with their toilette. Happily they listened as the high-spirited Cavaliers spoke of the successes of their king. Prince Rupert was to visit the castle on the morrow, and the two girls spent much time together, laughing, chatting and practising their curtseys.

With the Cavaliers stationed near the village, the young people dared to leave the castle and enjoy a sense of freedom as they mounted the opposite hill for the first time in many weeks. Dismayed they regarded the blackened grass scorched by the camp fires of the Roundheads. For a time their mood changed to one of sorrow as they discussed, with sadness, the tragedy of civil wars, with one brother fighting another, and one Englishman fighting another Englishman. But there was still relief and confidence in the presence of the Cavalier soldiers.

A banquet was in process of being prepared. Lady Mary clothed in grey and silver brocade, watched the arrangements with pride. The last remaining hens were killed for the feast, and soon Lady Bankes was seated with distinction at the head of the table among the host of Cavaliers, whose stylish hair was well curled, while jewelled, hilted swords protruded from their grand, lace trimmed coats. Proudly they drank a toast to King Charles and success to his Cause.

Repairs were commenced almost immediately; broken walls were mended, and the grass quickly grew outside. The little village of Corfe had been devastated, and work was begun on the church, looking scarred and lacking a roof – its restoration was a first aim and the many houses shattered or demolished.

While work on the castle and elsewhere was taking place, it was suggested that the family move to an old, uninhabited farmhouse nearby. Furniture and tapestry were sent there from Corfe Castle. Lady Bankes, the girls and other castle occupants would have a restful change of environment. Gleefully the company left for their temporary home, laughing and singing as they climbed the hill leading to it. After a short rest there was a joyful picnic dinner. In the cool of the evening, the party descended into Lulworth, getting their first breath of sea breeze and the first glimpse of a calm blue sea.

All slept well that night. Each day was a delight. Autumn colours had clothed the trees in gold and orange and reapers were busy among the golden corn. Sir John, with his son and friends, were active shooting game which was plentiful among the hills.

The contented party, more healthy and hopeful, as a result of their outside activities and change of scenery, often spoke of the King and his beloved Queen and hoped that the days of war would be ended before long.

In October 1643, it was decided they should all travel to Oxford where Charles and Henrietta kept their court, and where Dame Mary had the added pleasure of meeting her married daughter who was living in Oxford. More compliments were showered on the brave Dame for her courageous resistance.

The bitter war continued for another three years. The King, short of money, summoned Parliament to meet him at Oxford. By then, anger was strongly against him as he had levied huge sums and taxes without the consent of Parliament, but the Roundheads were also imposing taxes to carry on the war.

Despite the early victories of the King, the enemy was slowly winning. London and area had long been in their hands, while in the south, Weymouth, Dorchester,

Wareham, Lyme, Poole had been captured by the Roundheads. Corfe Castle was almost the only stronghold between Exeter and London which supported the royal cause.

In December 1644, Sir John died suddenly at Oxford, and Lady Bankes, back in Corfe Castle was again being besieged. Bravely she held out until the end of February 1646 when, through continued violent attacks and treachery, had to surrender without any offer of terms. The siege was commanded by Colonel Bingham, a descendant of a highly respected family in the county, and to show his admiration for the brave ladies, he preserved the lives of those in the castle. To salute the courage of Lady Bankes he allowed her to retain the keys of Corfe Castle, which today hang over the chimneypiece in the library of Kingston Lacy, an old royal estate which had been purchased by Sir John about 1634, and rebuilt by their son in 1664.

An order was given to demolish the castle, to make it untenable for military purposes. Stones of the walls and timbers from the roof were carried away, some were used to help rebuilt Dorset cottages. The rebels tried to uproot the walls but their thickness defied even gunpowder with which they attempted to blow up the castle. Eventually the castle was 'slighted' and left as a picturesque ruin. After the sequestration of the property, Lady Mary had to struggle to provide for her family and herself. All her beautiful tapestries, costly carpets and other valuable possessions fell into the hands of the enemy.

Lady Bankes lived to see the monarchy restored for a while with the accession of Charles II. When the sequestration was lifted a knighthood was bestowed on her eldest son, Ralph. She had already received the annual amount of her jointure from Cromwell, large sums having been paid by her to Parliament as a composition for herself and her children.

Lady Bankes last years were spent at Damory Court, Blandford, where she died on 11th April 1661. She was buried in the church at Ruislip, the family seat. The monument of white marble is inscribed: TO THE MEMORY OF LADY MARY BANKES . . . having had the honour to have borne with a constancy and courage above her sex a noble proportion of the late calamities, and the happiness to have outlived them so far as to have seen the restitution of the Government with great peace of mind laid down her most desired life. Leaving behind a record of her loyalty, constancy and courage which will live forever, deserving well the title of BRAVE DAME MARY.

Corfe Castle today

HENRIETTA TREGONWELL

Was she the REAL Founder of Bournemouth?

In the early days of Bournemouth, or Bourne, as it was then known, the names of the great landowners are well known, the Tapps Gervis Meyrick's, the Cooper Deans, Malmesbury's – all great families and linked with the ownership and development of Bournemouth. But what of their women? Little is heard about them. Take Lewis Tregonwell, the 'accepted' founder of Bournemouth. Portraits of him are to be seen in several municipal buildings, but what of Katherine, daughter and sole heiress of St. Barbe Sydenham, who died on the 14th February 1794, and Henrietta, his second wife, both extremely wealthy women? Henrietta, clever, talented and pretty, was the daughter of H.W. Portman of Orchard Portman and Bryanston, Blandford, Dorset. Lewis Tregonwell was the Squire of Cranborne Lodge, Deputy Lieutenant of Dorset, Captain of the Dorset Rangers who also assisted with the prevention of smuggling, during the period of the Napoleonic War.

After he retired from the army in 1810, Lewis and Henrietta spent some time in Mudeford, then a select sea-bathing area. Mrs. Tregonwell was unwell and grieving after the death of her baby son, Grosvenor in 1807, the day he should have been christened.

On a lovely afternoon in July 1810, her husband decided that a ride to the Bourne area that he knew so well would give her some pleasure. The area consisted of wild heathland, heather, swampy valleys, but there was the beauty of the sea and the empty golden sands. Mrs. Tregonwell was charmed with the beauty of the bay and suggested it would be ideal for a holiday residence near the sea. Lewis, happy to comply with a request that might restore her health, purchased 8½ acres from Sir George Ivison Tapps, the Lord of the Manor of Christchurch, for £179.11s. Would he have become the founder of Bourne without the suggestion from his wife? Who knows?

The first house was built, originally known as THE MANSION and today the Royal Exeter Hotel. A further house was built for their butler, known as Symes Cottage. Later the picturesque thatched cottage became known as Portman Lodge (after Mrs. Tregonwell's maiden name) – and where she lived after the death of her husband. Their time was divided between Cranborne and Bournemouth. Visitors and friends were invited when they were not in residence, which lead to the beginning of the letting system in Bourne. (The Marchioness of Exeter becoming the first tenant.)

The periods they spent in Bourne were happy ones, enjoying the recent pleasures of sea bathings and simple theatrical events. On Sundays they drove to Poole to attend services at St. James' Church, as there was then no church in Bournemouth. Tregonwell purchased more land at £40 per acre, then later at £60 per acre, their land being known as the Bourne Tregonwell Estate.

When Lewis died in 1832 he was buried in the family vault at Winterbourne Anderson, along with Grosvenor. His grieving wife had a cenotaph erected consisting of a huge pedestal, surmounted by an urn. The inscription read:

THIS URN
marks the favourite spot of
L.D.G. TREGONWELL,
The first proprietor resident
at Bournemouth
And to his beloved memory
is Dedicated
by his Widow, Henrietta,
Daughter of Henry William Portman Esq.,
1832

Unfortunately the monument disappeared many years ago.

Henrietta who proved to have both practical and business qualities was honoured to be asked to lay the foundation stone in 1841 for the commencement of a new church in Bournemouth, which became St, Peters, the Mother Church of Bournemouth, but bad weather and poor health prevented her from attending. When the new church was consecrated in 1845, Mrs. Tregonwell made arrangements for the bodies of her husband and son to be re-interred in a newly constructed vault there in February 1846. Two months later, Henrietta who had been suffering from illhealth for some time, died at Portman Lodge and was buried with her husband and child, in the pleasant spot she had chosen, near the top of the Thirty Nine steps, and where the large family grave can be seen today.

During her life she was often praised for her noble character, for her kind and generous works for charity and for her business acumen in the management of their estate after the death of her beloved husband. She was able to sell part of the estate for £800. an acre! Inflation – even in those days!

The Mansion

13

LADY JANE SHELLEY

– Daughter-in-Law of PERCY BYSSHE SHELLEY

JANE ST. JOHN was born on 24th February 1820, the daughter of Thomas Gibson. In 1841 she married the Hon. Charles Robert St. John, who, sadly, died three years later on 21st Jan. 1844. Jane had been an ardent admirer of Shelley, the man, and Shelley, the Romantic Poet. When some three years later she was staying with her sister in Chester Square, London, she was interested, and felt sympathy for, another widow who was living across the square. This was MARY WOLSTONECRAFT SHELLEY, author of Frankenstein, whose husband, PERCY BYSSHE SHELLEY, had been drowned in 1822, when sailing his boat between Leghorn and Lerici, Italy, and was caught in a tempestuous storm. Jane felt strongly that she would like to meet this other widow, but was too shy to introduce herself. But fate took a hand in matters.

Becoming friendly with a young man she met in Baden, she encouraged him to read and talk to her to prevent him from spending his time at the gaming tables. One day he remarked suddenly, "I wish you would do something for me."

To her astonishment, he continued, "I wish you would marry my best friend. His name is Sir Percy Florence Shelley and he is such a nice fellow, and you would suit each other capitally." The next step was taken by Mary, who had heard of Jane, and decided to visit her. From the outset Jane admired Mary, whom she described as a lovely being, with deep set eyes, a beautiful and clever women who had written Frankenstein when she was only 18 years old. When Jane met Sir Percy her admiration was carried on to the son of the poet, Shelley, whose mother had struggled through times of poverty to give him a good education. Admiration was mutual, with Mary describing Jane as the sweetest creature she had known, gentle and with a thousand other good qualities. "She has no taste for society, which will suit Percy who also likes a quiet life."

14

On 22nd June 1848, they were married at St. George's Church, Hanover Square. Jane realised how much Percy meant to his mother and that "she could not live without her boy." When they went abroad, they were accompanied by Mary. In Nice in 1850 they all spent a happy time together, with Percy and Jane painting and sketching, the beginning of a life of cultural leisure. Sir Percy shared his father's passion for sailing, was not interested in poetry, but enjoyed private theatricals, play writing, acting and scenery painting. In some ways he was a shy man, and in Jane he found a woman with charm of personality and an embracing sympathy. Mary wrote, "They suit each other so entirely, both being devoid of worldliness and worldly tastes. Both have cheerful tempers and affectionate hearts. Jane is the very ideal of women."

On the death of his grandfather, in 1844 Percy had inherited the title and the ancestral home, Field Place in Sussex, but the state of the building, its coldness and dampness, did not suit the health either of his wife or his mother, with the result that they looked for a new home. This they found in Boscombe, Bournemouth, among thick pine woods, deserted golden sands, a mainly tranquil sea, with cliffs, bracken and furze, reminding Sir Percy of his father's last home, Casa Magni, Lerici.

Land was cheap in the deserted, undeveloped Boscombe of those days and Sir Percy could have obtained the whole sea front from Boscombe Chine to what is now known as Southbourne, but he was content to purchase 400 acres with its unrivalled view of a tranquil sea. Boscombe Cottage, as it was then called, was the only building in the area, apart from two little thatched cottages and a wayside inn, known as The Ragged Cat, and today as Deacons. Boscombe Cottage, considerably enlarged, became the Boscombe Manor of today, attached to which, Sir Percy, that great lover of acting, had his own private theatre built. There he painted and designed scenery, spending many happy hours in his beloved theatre. It was said that the standard of his acting and that of Jane compared favourably with many professional actors of that time and that both of them could have made their names if they had appeared on the public stage.

Mary Shelley had already commenced to idealize Shelley, and after her death in 1851 Jane continued to idealize the romantic poet, often feeling as if she had really known him. Sir Percy could have his yachting and his theatre, but there was to be one room devoted to the life and works of the poet, and which became known as the Sanctum. In August 1878, Lady Shelley wrote to his friend, Edward Trelawny: "At Boscombe there is a room built expressly to receive all that we hold most sacred. One side is occupied by a niche in which is placed the life-sized model of the monument raised to the memory of Shelley and Mary by their son. The same room is never entered but by kindred feet, or by those in whose hearts Shelley lives – amongst other things, there is a glass case containing locks of hair. They belong to those, he and Mary valued as friends and with whom they had been most closely associated; Leigh Hunt, Byron, Edward Williams (who was drowned with Shelley) and one marked 'Trelawny 1822', it is as black as jet and was given at the time when Mary possessed in the giver a true and generous friend . . ."

The ceiling of the Sanctum was painted with stars, under which the children talked in whispers, mainly because of the relics of Shelley. There were two cases containing Shelley manuscripts, bound in green volumes. Under glass cases were some of the relics, a miniature of Shelley by Due de Montpensier, bracelets of Mary's hair and a miniature of their son, William, known as Willmouse. Lady Jane had created a devoted shrine to her father-in-law. There was the copy of Sophocles and Keats found in the pockets of the dead man.

Standing upright on the mantlepiece were Etruscan and Greek figures and tear bottles. Over them was a painting of Mary Shelley, by Rothwell, now on show in the

National Portrait Gallery. There was also an unfinished portrait of the poet, by Miss Curran. Above all, his heart was kept in the Sanctum, which had been snatched by Trelawny from his funeral pyre. Previously this had been kept by Mary in a silken bag inside the pages of Shelley's 'Adonais', and in the part of the poem which speaks of immortality.

Owing to forged letters, unreliable biographies of the poet, whose reputation was one of ill-repute, it became important to Sir Percy and Lady Shelley to obtain a good biographer. The Shelley legend became the life's work of Lady Jane. All false statements, frivolous remarks, his various love affairs and his radical political views were to be removed.

In Shelley's friend, Jefferson Hogg, she considered she had found her ideal biographer. His literary works and early knowledge of the poet seemed to indicate that he would be the most fitting person to write of Shelley's life. In 1857 Hogg came to Boscombe and was entrusted with some of their precious documents. But Hogg proved incapable of giving an accurate account; he either belittled Shelley or claimed that he was divine. The books were full of inaccuracies and muddled descriptions. When Sir Percy and Lady Shelley saw the first two volumes of an intended four volumes, they were dismayed and horrified, especially as they had actually chosen Hogg. Lady Shelley, greatly distressed at the fantastic caricature of her wonderful father-in-law managed to persuade her easy-going husband to forego his main interests of yachting in 'The Wren', named after one of Lady Shelley's nicknames, and writing and acting in plays at their own theatre, to retrieve the documents and manuscripts from their 'so-called' friend, which he did.

To another friend, Leigh Hunt, Sir Percy wrote that Hogg had produced the most disgusting book that can be conceived, and he condemned Hogg as a narrow-minded and unsympathetic creature. This unfortunate episode resulted in Lady Shelley herself becoming an author and writing THE SHELLEY MEMORIALS in 1859. In them she praised the poet's fine reputation and denied the lies and inaccuracies written by Hogg. She also wrote that from their materials a book was produced which shocked those who had the greatest rights to form an opinion of Shelley.

Lady Shelley was again distressed when she heard that the poet's tomb in Rome was becoming badly neglected. With her husband, in 1863, they journeyed to Rome. On arrival, they found to their great pleasure that the grave was in perfect order, with roses and violets in flower all around it. On enquiry, they were informed that the grave had been beautified by the order of a young Englishman, who visited it with two ladies. Twelve years later Lady Shelley discovered that the young man was Alfred Austin, the future poet laureate. In a letter to him she wrote "We have one more wish now – to clasp your hand and thank you face to face." Later they were able to meet.

The grave of Shelley was indicated by a flat stone. But it was not until 1891 that Jane decided to have a large monument erected, for which she commissioned Onslow Ford, the sculptor. The massive work portrayed the naked, white body of the poet, beautiful in appearance, and, supporting it, a bronze base ornamented with the Muse of Poetry. There was much criticism of the huge statue, but Jane's opinion was that she wanted to prevent the Italians who had threatened to raise an even larger one. Arguments arose about the ownership of the grave and the size of the statue, which would have extended to the grave of Trelawny. An amicable settlement arose when Lady Shelley agreed to place her monument elsewhere but on condition that no alterations would be made to the tomb.

In December 1891, Lady Shelley wrote to the Master of University College, Oxford, offering them the monument to Percy Bysshe Shelley, a former member of their college (from which he had been expelled for his views on atheism), and with £500 towards expenses, and on condition that it was placed in a suitable position and light. The Memorial was accepted with gratefulness by the Master and Dons of Oxford. Times had changed and his genius as an outstanding poet, had, by then, been recognized. In June 1893, the Memorial was opened in the presence of Heads of the College and other important persons, including the sculptor and Lady Shelley. The latter happily declared that for 40 years she had endeavoured to portray the true nobleness of Shelley's character, and that if he made mistakes the love and respect of people should not be taken away. The Master, in his reply, referred to the great poet who was prophetic in all directions of what was to come to the world.

Shelley's last home, Casa Magni, Lerici, attracted many of his former friends and admirers, who came, as on a pilgrimage, to the shabby, white house standing on the beach, and where the sea in its wild moods rushed onto the ground floor. When Sir Percy and Lady Shelley visited there, Lady Shelley who had spiritualistic beliefs spent a night in the poet's bedroom, hoping to see his ghost, but to her disappointment, nothing was seen. It was many years later that claims were made that a tall, slender figure, in the likeness of the poet, had been seen entering the room. Sir Percy had thought of buying the villa, but when the landlord realised he was talking to the son of the poet, he raised the price so much, that purchase was impossible. There they met an old sailor, who kissed Sir Percy's feet declaring emotionally "He was fair, he was beautiful. He was like Jesus Christ. I carried him in my arms through the water." Lady Jane remembered this new tale and was always pleased to recount it.

Between 1884 and 1887 Sir Percy and Lady Shelley became very friendly with the invalid writer, Robert Louis Stevenson and his devoted wife, Fanny, who were then living in Bournemouth. Lady Shelley, especially, became devoted to Louis and even looked upon him as her own son, seeing a strong likeness in him to the poet. Fanny was to describe Lady Shelley as 'delicious,' "but no longer young, suffering from the effects of a terrible accident that has left her a hopeless invalid, but with all the fire of youth and ready to plunge into any wild extravagance at a moment's notice."

Sir Percy and Lady Shelley had no children of their own, but adopted Lady Shelley's niece, Bessie Florence Gibson, when she was a child. When Bessie married, living nearby, she brought her children often to Boscombe Manor. One of her daughters, wrote of Lady Shelley, when she was an old lady, "To the end (Lady Jane died in 1899) she retained her extraordinary vitality in which lay one of the secrets of her great charm. She was intensely alive and delighted in living. She was short and stout like most of her family. Her eyes were grey, hazel, with thick, white, silver hair, She had worn her hair short since a yachting accident in 1870 which had twisted her neck and caused her great pain. On her little finger she wore a cameo ring which had belonged to Percy Bysshe Shelley which she valued more than all her possessions."

Lady Shelley, still not happy about a biography that would do justice to the poet, had, by 1882 written a four-volume book, SHELLEY AND MARY, based on selected manuscripts and Shelley papers in her possession. Originally only twelve copies were printed privately which were not to be published until 30 years after her death. A preface was written by Sir Percy: "These volumes, containing 1,243 pages, have been prepared for the press by Lady Shelley, with the object of preserving from destruction precious records in her possession."

In 1886, 64 years after the death of the poet, an approved biography was published, by Edward Dowden, a Professor of English Literature, which remained the standard work for many years. Dowden's work was carefully scrutinized by Lady Shelley, but he always admitted that he had received much help from her and access to the many documents at Boscombe Manor.

Sir Percy and Lady Shelley, besides their cultural interests, played an active part in fostering the progress of the developing Boscombe, at one time considered a rival to the growing Bournemouth. When an application was made to the Bournemouth Commissioners for a pier in Boscombe, they met with little success, resulting in the formation of a private Pier Company, with Sir Percy and other important landowners in charge. In October 1888 there was great jubilation as Lady Shelley fixed the first pile, which weighed about one ton, and had been placed in position under a wooden capstan, around which was fixed a band of stout rope linked to a seven horse-power steam engine. The engine was started by means of a red silk ribbon, which was pulled by Lady Shelley. Loud cheers followed the ceremony, while on many roads strings of flags appeared with colourful mottoes: PROSPERITY TO BOSCOMBE, LONG LIVE SIR PERCY AND LADY SHELLEY.

After the death of Sir Percy in 1889, Lady Shelley lived quietly for the next ten years, until her death in 1899, devoting more and more time to the preservation and sorting of the Shelley memoranda, rejecting those she considered unfavourable to the poet, and obtaining more documents.

If PERCY BYSSHE SHELLEY had been alive, he could not have found two more devoted women than his wife, MARY WOLSTONECRAFT SHELLEY and his daughter-in-law LADY JANE SHELLEY, who spent most of their lives in ensuring that the world were aware of the genius of the poet, and that his reputation was far greater than in the days when he was drowned in 1822.

When Lady Shelley died in 1899, all the documents and Shelley memorabilia, so lovingly kept at Boscombe Manor, were divided between her heir, Shelley Scarlett, the Bodleian Library in Oxford, and Sir Percy's cousin, Edward, heir to the baronetcy.

In the centre of Bournemouth, in St. Peter's Churchyard, is the famous Shelley family grave, standing out on a slope, white and dominant.

Here are buried – MARY WOLLSTONECRAFT SHELLEY, d. 1851, the second wife of Percy Bysshe Shelley, the mother of Sir Percy Florence Shelley and the author of Frankenstein and other books. Her body was brought there from Chester Place, London, where she died. Her parents, WILLIAM GODWIN and MARY WOLLSTONECRAFT GODWIN, radical free thinkers, were originally buried in St. Pancras Cemetery, but after Parliament authorized the building of a railway through the churchyard, their bodies were brought to Bournemouth to be laid besides their daughter. When Sir Percy died in 1889, the heart of his father, so carefully preserved in the Sanctum by Lady Shelley, was buried with him in the famous grave. Last, but by no means least, the devoted daughter-in-law was laid to rest there in 1899 by the side of those she had cherished so dearly.

MRS. ROBERT LOUIS STEVENSON

– formerly FANNY VAN DE GRIFT OSBOURNE

How often is it said that behind a successful man is a good woman and this could not be more true than in the case of Robert Louis Stevenson and his happy marriage with Fanny van de Grift Osbourne.

Robert Louis Stevenson was born in Edinburgh on November 13th 1850. From his nurse, mother, highland ancestors, came his great love of Scottish romances. His whole life was a fight against ill-health with many travels abroad searching for a cure in the sun for consumption.

On a visit to France to visit his artist cousin, Bob Stevenson, he passed many happy hours in the artists' colony at Barbizon, near Fontainbleau. But when he returned there in 1876, he was annoyed to hear that the area, sacred to men, had been invaded by a woman. Curious, besides being horrified, he hastened to nearby Montigny and on to the inn where this unknown female was staying. In the lamplight he caught sight of Fanny, and later confessed that it was love at first sight through the window. Excitedly he entered the room to meet the lady. Mrs. Osbourne, living apart from her husband, had come to France for peace and partly to study art and educate her children, a daughter of seventeen and two boys. The younger, aged five, had recently died in Paris and the mother was still grieving, but the lively and talkative Scot suddenly gave life a new zest. She was then in her 37th year and Louis was in his 26th, but the age difference was never a hindrance. Quickly they became good friends and then more than friends.

Fanny van de Grift had been married when she was 17 to a good looking youth of 20 who proved to have a too-easy disposition and attraction to other women. Fanny was of Swedish-Dutch extraction but her relations on both sides for many generations had been American. She was small, square, with black hair and a dusky complexion, while her dark eyes could flash in anger or melt in pity.

After an arranged canoe trip with Sir Walter Simpson, he returned with eager impatience to Grez where Mrs. Osbourne was waiting for him. In the lively company of Louis and his friends, Fanny began to forget her many troubles. Louis, knowing that his strict Calvinistic parents would disapprove of this new friendship, his companions were sworn to secrecy. They were able to pass many pleasant days, discussing, reading poetry, while Fanny often relaxed contentedly swinging in a hammock in the grounds. There were canoeing contests, studies of French peasant life and manners, improvised dances and theatrical entertainments. Later that year he left Fanny and his artistic friends and returned to Edinburgh. As he had previously qualified as a Barrister at Edinburgh University, he had a vague idea of practising at the bar as his father opposed his real wish of becoming a writer – but he received few briefs. There were more visits to London, France and more meetings with Fanny. Often he was in mental torment as the woman he loved belonged to another, even though her husband had deserted her.

From California came the news that Mrs. Osbourne had returned there to institute divorce proceedings, but owing to the strain and worry had become ill. As his father objected to his proposed marriage, he decided to leave home without explaining his intentions. In August 1879 he sailed for New York where he arrived in drenching rain and with very little money. With difficulty he obtained work as a junior reporter at 2 dollars a week, and also when he moved on to San Francisco. Besides being poor, he was ill, emaciated, with a ghastly pale face; lacking money he was unable to get treatment.

In Monterey where Mrs. Osbourne was living with her family, Louis became a daily visitor. Mr. Samuel Osbourne, Fanny's ex-husband who had a Government appointment, was willing to help her financially, to grant her her liberty, and was agreeable to supporting her until her next marriage – but then he lost his post and was unable to aid further.

Although poverty stricken, by January 1880 Louis had become engaged to the woman he had loved for 3½ years. Fanny was already directing and superintending his work. When Louis thought of writing a modern-type work DON JUAN, she disapproved – he must edify and entertain, but not shock. In March, due to worry and starvation he collapsed with galloping consumption and a burning fever. Fanny, full of concern, was able to nurse him, though she began to think there was little hope of saving his life. Then a miracle happened, and the man thought to be dying, did not die. His spirits arose and much of his recovery was attributed to his loving nurse. News of his financial and health problems reached his family in Edinburgh, with the result he was promised £250 a year.

When Fanny's divorce proceedings were over, she wished to postpone the marriage for another year, but Stevenson, who had travelled over land and sea to join her again, refused. On 19th May 1880 they were married despite his poor health. Many people considered she was marrying a doomed man – he was so thin and had a dreadful cough. As his Doctor did not expect him to live more than a few months, it was thought to be an act of valour on her part. But Louis' thoughts began to turn to his family in Scotland with a strong wish to return home. In August 1880 they arrived in Britain. Mrs. Stevenson was filled with fear at the thought of meeting his parents, particularly Louis' stern, calvinistic father. For Louis' sake she was determined to make a good impression and, to her delight, found that they agreed on many subjects and soon she had developed a close affection with Mr. Stevenson Senr. He was captivated by the clever and sensible woman his son had married, with a character as strong and romantic as that of Louis. Her exquisite tact and understanding brought Louis back into affection which had not existed between him and his family for some time. There were family holidays in the mountains in the Grampians and in Davos, Switzerland, for the benefit of Louis' health.

On their return to Scotland in 1884, there were discussions with his physician as to whether the English climate in summer would be warm enough. He was becoming tired of travelling.

It was decided that Bournemouth would be the most suitable, and where his step-son, Lloyd Osbourne, was at school. Despite his suffering, Louis was happy in Bournemouth, among its heath and pine trees which made him think of Scotland, and where there were sunny crannies where he could rest. They spent three months in a boarding house on the West Cliff, 'Wensleydale' and then moved to a furnished house situated among the pinewoods of Branksome, 'Bonalie Towers.' As Louis' health seemed to improve, his father, Thomas, bought a house in Bournemouth which he presented to his dear daughter-in-law, with £500 for furnishings. They named the house 'Skerryvore' to honour his father and the family firm who had constructed the lighthouse, Skerryvore, off the Argyll coast. But Louis' health slowly worsened, and in Bournemouth he passed three years of chronic invalidism and seclusion, but with amazing literary activity, much of it carried out in bed, and on occasions not even allowed to speak.

Despite Louis' sickness, haemorrhages, their three years in Bournemouth, their last years in this country, was mainly a period of happiness. They obtained great pleasure from their yellow, brick House, on the edge of Alum Chine, with blue slate roof and among laurels and rhododendrons. The garden merged into a network of paths, deeply wooded, leading down to the sea. Fanny loved the garden and made it her special charge. She was also a good house manager. She could paint and decorate, and with her son, Lloyd, was mainly responsible for installing the fine Sheraton furniture in the 'blue' room, blue china and many paintings. When Louis was well enough he would sit at the foot of the table, always smoking. Fanny would sit opposite him, who has been described as the tutelary genius of Skerryvore and of a heroic mould. Beneath a placid and often vivacious exterior, there was concealed much suffering and before which many women would have broken down.

According to Adelaide A. Boodle, who became a firm friend, and was also referred to as their GAMEKEEPER as she looked after their collection of animals and birds when they were away from the house, Mrs. Stevenson was the kindest person she had known. She pitied those in trouble and rarely condemned anyone, but could be wild with fury at cruelty. Her tenderness shone from her eyes. To Louis, she was 'his critic on the hearth' of whom he was so proud and was also dependent on her good advice. He considered her critical faculties far greater than his own and always listened for her judgement.

Their many discussions were frank and open. On talking of the death of either of them, Fanny had said that it would be impossible for her to live without him. His reply was that she must live to see his biography written and particularly it had to be revised by her.

Throughout Louis' many problems in Bournemouth, he worked almost unceasingly. Needing money, he searched for a story that he could write quickly. The idea is said to have come to him partially in a dream. One night, in his sleep, he cried out in horror. Fanny, scared, woke him up quickly, but he immediately protested, "Why did you awake me? I was dreaming a fine bogy-tale." And in the morning he exclaimed excitedly, "I have got my shilling shocker. I dreamed that a man was being pressed into a cabinet when he swallowed a drug which changed him into another being." The story which became famous as DR. JEKYLL AND MR. HYDE was also influenced by the life of Deacon Brodie, a respected councillor during the day and a criminal at night.

The first draft was dashed off by Louis in a frenzy of excitement, but when he read it to Fanny, to his surprise, she condemned it outright as an allegory made into a rather commonplace story. A violent and noisy argument followed. Stevenson lost his temper when, suddenly, to his wife's consternation, he hurled the manuscript into the fire, seemingly in a passion, but in reality to indicate that she, as usual, was right, and that it must be remodelled and re-written. A second version was produced at 'white heat,' and again re-written. It was actually printed within ten weeks in 1886 – overcoming the threat of bankruptcy. In six months 40,000 copies had been sold. While in Bournemouth he also wrote A CHILD'S GARDEN OF VERSE, 1885, MORE ARABIAN NIGHTS. 1886 MERRY MEN and UNDERWOODS 1887.

Periods of illness continued. Fanny too, became unwell, mainly caused by worrying about her husband. Although a brilliant conversationalist, she was also a good listener. Louis often read aloud to her, waiting for her criticism. Often her smile was sad, but she showed infinite patience and self-restraint. He must be guarded from every risk, even if it meant being unpleasant to visitors who stayed too long, and no one with a cold was allowed to come near him.

Worsening health meant another move to a warmer climate. There was great sadness in both their hearts when they left their ivy-clad house by the attractive, well-wooded chine, in August 1887. Although Louis had lived there 'like a weevil in a biscuit' he was able to welcome a few special friends, and limited his outside visits mainly to Boscombe Manor, the home of Sir Percy and Lady Shelley (the son and daughter-in-law of the famous, romantic poet, Percy Bysshe Shelley.'

After leaving Bournemouth, they stayed in winter quarters for consumptives near the shores of Saranac Lake in America until April 1888. In that year, still searching for better health, they settled in Samoa in the South Seas, where Louis died suddenly in 1894 from the rupture of a blood vessel in the brain.

Fanny, greatly distressed by the suddenness of her husband's death, was ill for a time. Later she was able to leave New York where she had been staying, and returned to England. There, as discussed during those happy days in Bournemouth, she was able to assist Mr. Sidney Colvin, their friend, who was engaged in writing the LIFE OF STEVENSON. It was left for Mrs. Stevenson to decide what should be put in the book and what should be omitted.

Fanny survived her husband by 20 years. She had returned to California, and there, at Santa Barbara on February 18th 1914 died, as suddenly as Louis, and like him from the bursting of a blood vessel in the brain. She was cremated and later the casket was taken to Apia in the South Sea islands, and built into the side of his tomb at Mt. Vera.

Robert Louis Stevenson was one of the great writers of the 19th century but in admiring the works of the man and his tremendous fight against ill health, let us not forget the wonderful woman who devoted so much of her life to him, and, but for her care and love, could not have lived as long as he did.

Robert Louis Stevenson

EMMA LAVINIA GIFFORD

– THE FIRST MRS. THOMAS HARDY

How sad that the love affair and marriage between Thomas Hardy and Emma Lavinia Gifford should have slowly turned to one of bitterness, lack of communication and even hatred. How strange too, that after Emma's death in 1912, Hardy, filled with remorse for his neglect of Emma, should have been inspired to write some of his finest and most acclaimed poetry about his departed wife, again causing unhappiness and loneliness to his second wife, Florence Dugdale.

Emma was born in Plymouth in 1840. She loved the bustling town, with its busy sea port, and many opportunities for cultural activities, social events and entertainments. Members of her family could sing or play instruments, and Emma had an attractive singing voice. She always declared that her twenty years in Plymouth were the happiest of her life, although the four years' courtship by Hardy were also times of pleasure. Her father, a Solicitor, unfortunately drank excessively. His mother, who loved him dearly, on discovering that he did not care for his work, supported the family from her own money, content that her son should be a gentleman of leisure.

The family, with its professional and church background, believed in gentility and good breeding, so Emma, throughout her life, was conscious of the importance of status and background. On the death of her grandmother, the family discovered, to their horror, that she had been supporting them from her own capital, and not from a permanent income as they had thought, and that there was very little money left. Hastily, almost surreptitiously, they moved to Bodmin in Cornwall, where the many enjoyable activities of Plymouth were unheard of among its country folk.

About this time Emma was described as having a high colour, heavy jaw, narrow eyes and fair hair. She was vivacious and a chatter-box. Her sister, Helen, to whom she was devoted, was as dark as Emma was fair.

When Helen was 30 she accepted a proposal of marriage from Reverend Caddell Holder, who was 65, a widower with grandchildren, who had recently been given the parish of St. Juliot in North Cornwall. Rather surprisingly, Emma accompanied the two newly-weds, staying with them for several years, until her own marriage. The tiny village proved even more uninspiring than Bodmin, and among the primitive country folk, the two sisters found little in common. Emma's boredom was relieved by the gift of a horse from some friends. Not able to walk much because of lameness from birth, she enjoyed riding briskly along country lanes, and even daringly by the edges of cliffs. She was able to assist her brother-in-law by visiting parishioners in outlying districts.

It was at St. Juliot that she met Thomas Hardy in 1870. She was then 30 and marriage prospects were poor in the isolated village. Almost immediately she was attracted to this young man, who had actually spent five years in London and could be said to be a man of the world. Soon Emma, who was intensely religious, felt that Hardy was divinely intended for her by God and that he was her man of destiny.

Thomas Hardy was born at Higher Bockhampton, Dorset, in 1840 in a small thatched cottage, where his father, from humble beginnings, had become a master mason. Thomas, at birth, was thought to be still-born and put on one side, until the midwife realised that there was some life in the child.

Throughout his life he had periods of morbid depression, sometimes even wishing he was actually dead. In the cottage he lived with his parents, grandmother, a brother and two sisters. From his mother, Jemima, a strong minded woman who had great influence on her family, and from his grandmother, Tom heard exciting tales of village life. His receptive mind was influenced by the dramas, tragedies, hangings and death so that his writings reflected a true feeling for the country around him. After leaving school, Hardy was apprenticed to a local architect, and then became an assistant to a noted firm of church restorers in London. There, he met many interesting characters, enjoyed the theatre, opera, picture galleries, and even visited night-clubs. It was rumoured that he became friendly with an unknown H.A. who has always remained a mystery. Throughout his life, despite his gloom and doom thoughts, he was susceptible to attractive, young women. There were romantic friendships with his cousins, Rebecca and Martha Sparkes, followed by a much more serious affair with their younger sister, Tryphena, who was 11 years younger than Hardy. It was said that he even bought her a ring, but marriage between cousins was very much discouraged at that time.

On being sent to St Juliot to make plans and drawings towards the restoration of the church to prevent further deterioration, he was received and welcomed by a vivacious blond, Emma. (Her brother-in-law was ill and Helen was attending to his requirements). A happy time soon developed for both, with picnics and excursions along leafy, country lanes, Emma often riding on horseback and Tom walking besides her. As they savoured the beauty of majestic cliffs and swirling seas, they discovered they shared a love of music, poetry and books. There were frequent visits to St. Juliot by Hardy, with long intervals of absence in between. It is thought that these infrequent visits did not allow them to know each other as they really were, or to realise at that time that there were serious differences in their characters. Even then Hardy was becoming agnostic in his beliefs, while Emma always remained a devout Protestant and with a hatred of Catholicism.

Many letters passed between the two lovers which further created the romantic, idyllic atmosphere. In one letter Emma wrote that all around her seemed as in a vision, and their love the only reality. Unfortunately, for future biographers, many of these letters were burnt after Emma's death. But Emma was content, even feeling that she had seen Hardy before in her dreams. In this tiny village there had been no one of her standing, so Hardy stood out as a most desirable person, especially as she, too, was trying to write. Neither of them had had anything published at that time. Perhaps, subconsciously, he was her last chance to get away from the rural backwater.

Hardy had written poetry over a period of time, but it was as a prose writer of mainly Dorset and Wessex stories that he made his name. His first attempt, DESPERATE REMEDIES, published anonymously, was eventually accepted, after alterations, when Emma kindly offered to make him a fair copy of the work. This marked the beginning of her involvement with his work, and from this time, 1870, she assisted him with research, made notes and corrected copy. Her happiness increased as she helped Tom, making herself more indispensable to the man she admired so much. Much later, when some people thought she had actually written some of the works, she rarely undeceived them, but basked in the glory.

As Emma was proud of her genteel and professional background, Hardy began to be self-conscious about his own family and relatives, with their countrified appearance and broad Dorset accents, and said as little as possible about them.

In 1871, his third visit to supervise the start of work on the church Emma was delighted to lay the foundation stone of the new tower and north aisle.

When UNDER THE GREENWOOD TREE was published anonymously, Hardy received £20. It was thought that the heroine was based on his previous love, Tryphena. Shortly afterwards the story was serialised, for which he received the more acceptable sum of £200. It was about this time that Emma urged him to give up architecture for the uncertainty of writing. When he wrote A PAIR OF BLUE EYES, the first to bear his real name, both Emma and his experiences of Cornwall came into the book.

When their respective parents knew of their intention to be married, none of them were pleased, while Emma's father was violently opposed. Hardy was not considered good enough for the hand of his daughter. He even referred to Hardy as a 'low-born churl'. Emma was unaware then of his many past 'amours' with young ladies, which were to continue throughout his life.

On 17th September, 1874, after over four years' courtship, Hardy and Emma were married at St. Peter's Church, Paddington, by Emma's uncle, Canon Edwin Hamilton Gifford, who ten years later was to become Archdeacon of London. Much later, Emma was to refer with pride to her uncle, and his religion, as a contrast to her ungodly husband. Only two members of her family were present at the wedding and none of his.

From Brighton, where they passed a few nights, en route for France Hardy informed his brother Henry, that they were married, telling him to let the family know – their first knowledge of the wedding.

On return from their honeymoon in France, they obtained rooms in Surbiton, which Emma found depressing after the excitement and gaiety of Paris but where they stayed for 5½ months. In March 1875 they moved nearer the West End.

In November, FAR FROM THE MADDING CROWD was published with favourable reviews and good sales, and a request for a serial in Cornhill Magazine. This was followed by ETHELBERTA, a comedy, which included some of his own experiences, and also notes taken from Emma's diary.

A move to Swanage lasted ten months. There Emma wrote her first unpublished novel, MAID OF THE SHORE. Although it had the faults of a first time writer, Hardy did not then, or at any time, try to help her, although he gladly assisted other literary lady friends. It was while staying there that Emma met his two sisters, Mary and Kate for the first time, when all seemed quite friendly. Later she was to meet Hardy's parents, but there seems to be no record of their first meeting.

In March 1876 they moved to Yeovil house hunting, which proved unsuccessful, so off they went abroad again, visiting several countries in Europe. Even in the early stages of marriage, Hardy could be inconsiderate, and despite Emma's lameness, he tired her out by taking her over the battlefields of Waterloo, a distance of several miles, and the following day taking her on another long walk to a lace making factory. At the end of the visit abroad Emma wrote pathetically in her diary, 'Going back to England where we have no home and no chosen county.'

Their first real home was at Riverside Villa, Sturminster Newton. Emma was by that time 36, and although they both loved children, and dearly would have liked to have their own, it was becoming less likely. This was said to be the happiest time of their married life. They were welcomed by the Dashwoods who owned most of Sturminster Newton, and they met other society people. There was dancing on the green, excursions, boating on the river and other activities. Because of Hardy's work, Emma interested herself in the history of Sturminster. She was writing poetry and also had ambitions of becoming a writer. Emma had not realised that there would be times when she would be alone, while Hardy was engrossed in writing or visiting new friends by himself. By then Emma had learned, with dismay, of Hardy's agnostic views, though he would still attend church with her.

A first visit to Bockhampton was not a success, Emma being conscious of her social superiority, but the following August they actually stayed at the cottage, when they enjoyed excursions, with Hardy's Mother, Jemima, to Portland and other parts of Dorset. Emma's feelings of loneliness increased as Hardy became more immersed in his work and contacting people who would be useful to him; even then a feeling of tension seemed to have entered their marriage.

In 1878 they left Sturminster for London, Hardy feeling it was important for him to be in the centre of activities, while Emma wondered if London would bring them closer together, and that she would be able to share more of his activities. Dancing or playing games was difficult for her because of her lameness, with the result that she put on weight, becoming quite dumpy. Hardy, dining with his publishers and other literary celebrities, seemed blind to his wife's loneliness and the fact that their lives were beginning to separate.

There was a period in Weymouth the following year where Hardy was getting material for THE TRUMPET MAJOR which was serialised in 'Good Words' magazine. Hardy who had always been a weakly youth, began to suffer from various health problems; a visit to France brought no improvement. Emma looked after him and nursed him devotedly, as he also went through a period of morbid thoughts and strange fantasies. Back in Tooting, London, his health deteriorated further. It was not until Macmillan's friends sent for their own Doctor that internal bleeding, caused by a stone in the bladder, was diagnosed. He was informed that he should either have an operation or lie in bed for a period with his feet higher than his head. As the first editions of his serial A LAODI-CEAN had been printed, an operation would prevent him from further instal-ments, and he could lose a well-paid contract. For nearly five months he lay on his back, often in great pain. Emma happily agreed to write out the story from his dictation, in addition to nursing and caring for him. Despite his illness he made many useful contacts, and even felt attracted to an actress, Helen Mathews, who reminded him of Tryphena. Despite her careful nursing, the estrangement between them seemed to increase, partly caused by Emma's strong religious views and her feelings of superiority.

To improve his health, they moved to Wimborne in 1883, where they stayed for two years. There he wrote TWO ON A TOWER, several short stories and poems. Together they explored the countryside looking for Dorset features to incorporate into his stories, while Emma made a list of real and Hardy's own Wessex names.

FAR FROM THE MADDING CROWD brought Hardy both fame and acclaim and the recognition that he was a first-rate writer. The book was followed by a stage adaption in Liverpool in 1882 at which they were both welcomed and treated as most important guests.

But Emma had a poor opinion of his family and of his relatives in PUDDLE-TOWN, so there were difficulties again. HARDY, who was well aware of Emma's views, and who was meeting important people from a higher strata of society, also began to feel ashamed of his countrified relatives. His feelings were often confused and mixed, as he was always more content and felt better, when in his beloved Dorset.

Becoming more wealthy, Hardy decided to chose and design a large brick house, near Dorchester, which he called 'Maxgate', and was built by brother, Henry. Although the house was in a bleak and remote area, was dark, gloomy and even damp, Hardy was pleased with it, its gardens and nearby woods, and where he could spend long hours in his studio working. Like a true Victorian husband, Emma was not consulted about his decision to live near Dorchester, and where he would also be much nearer his strong-willed, ambitious mother, Jemima.

Poor Emma, she had never liked the country, and felt depressed and unhappy about the move, and also did not like the nearness to his family. Her gloom and the gloomy house even began to affect Hardy, who besides having periods of depression, suffered from sick headaches and the bladder trouble which plagued him most of his life. Emma, often hurt by his continuing friendships with bright, well known and attractive, younger women, became more eccentric. In an attempt to win him back, she started wearing unsuitable and younger styles of clothes, although by then she had a middle-aged appearance, and was portly.

Mrs. Robert Louis Stevenson, after a visit with her famous husband described Hardy as a pale, gentle, frightened man with an ugly wife, while Gertrude

Atherton, a novelist, described Emma as a plain, high-stomached woman with hair tightly drawn back. The impression was often given that she was more proud of being an Archdeacon's niece, than that she was the wife of the famous Thomas Hardy. Emma could never forget his humble beginnings and that he was just a poor clerk when she met him.

Becoming more bitter, she was known to belittle and discourage him. So many of his views offended her, particularly his views on religion. T. O'Connor referred to her as Hardy's evil genius, while a Mrs. Sheridan considered that she led Hardy a hell of a life and was also half-cracked. One visitor considered her a devil, although others commented on her kindness and welcome. But if visitors asked especially for Hardy, she would say that he was not there, or not available.

Despite a more limited contact and communication with each other, there were compensations. Disappointed that they had had no children of their own, they enjoyed visitors' children, who often played in their large garden. Emma particularly loved gardening, and was often followed by her devoted cats – four of them. Lilian and Gordon Gifford, children of Emma's brother, Walter, often stayed at Maxgate, and were practically adopted by Hardy and Emma. Their education was paid for by Hardy, who also introduced Gordon to architecture and arranged an apprenticeship with his old firm, Blomfields.

By the 1880s Hardy had finished the MAYOR OF CASTERBRIDGE, and started on THE WOODLANDERS, and also on TESS OF THE d'URBERVILLES, while Emma, at this time, was still assisting her husband.

Hardy's output was amazing. By 1910 he had written 15 novels, several short stories, an epic drama, THE DYNASTS, three volumes of poetry, and numerous articles. He was awarded ORDER OF MERIT by King Edward VII, and also given the FREEDOM OF DORCHESTER. This latter gave him more satisfaction than any of his other awards, especially as Dorchester had been slow to recognise they had a man of genius in their midst.

Despite the tensions between Hardy and Emma, they still had a long holiday together in Italy, and when three men attempted to rob Hardy, Emma, noticing them, cried out aloud and rushed towards the men who quickly disappeared.

About 1890 Emma began keeping her BLACK DIARIES of denouncing Hardy in the harshest terms, and also WHAT I THINK OF MY HUSBAND, in which she expressed her hurt and bitterness. These contrast with HER RECOLLECTIONS which were also written at a time of estrangement, but still described in pleasant tones her life up to and including meeting Hardy at St. Juliot.

By 1892, TESS was published, and although it received criticism for immorality, over 20,000 copies were sold making Hardy even more wealthy.

The following year they were invited to Dublin to stay with Lord Houghton, Viceroy of Ireland, a widower, whose sister, Florence Henniker, acted as hostess for him. Florence, aged 38, handsome, good looking, had written three published novels. Hardy, almost immediately, felt himself strongly attracted to the younger woman. In letters to her he addressed her as 'My dear fellow scribbler', and felt that there should be stronger feelings than just friendship. But Florence, married woman, also deeply religious, welcomed Hardy's friendship and assistance with writing, but would not allow it to go further, even though she was willing to go to London with him to see Ibsen's MASTER BUILDER, and also to one or two other places.

Emma, again hurt over this new friendship, gradually became more and more eccentric. Hardy had never assisted Emma with her writing, but was more than willing to help Florence and other young, literary ladies, which by then included two American sisters, Catherine and Rebekah Owen. Rebekah, the youngest, was a devoted admirer of Hardy and his works, almost worshipping her hero. During this time he was dramatising TESS, working on JUDE THE OBSCURE, and also socialising with elegant and admiring young ladies, resulting in Emma becoming stranger and more jealous. Hardy too, was hurt at times that Emma was not proud of his success as a writer, and he felt that she no longer cared for him.

When JUDE was published in Harpers in 1895, there was much criticism. Disliked intensely by Emma for its mockery of religion, she was said to have visited Dr. Garnett, Keeper of Printed Books at the Museum to urge him to stop the publication of the book owing to its evil views, and also suggested that the manuscript should be burnt. She told Hardy that she would have nothing more to do with any of his works. For 24 years she had assisted him, By then he was not unduly worried as he had contacts with innumerable literary and intellectual ladies. Critics called the book, JUDE THE OBSCENE, HARDY THE DEGENER-ATE, DIRT, DRIVEL. The Bishop of Wakefield was so disgusted that he threw his copy on the fire – but still 20,000 copies were sold. Hardy, upset, by the continuous criticism, vowed to write no further novels and to return to his first love of poetry. Aged 55, a wealthy man and a well known writer, he was welcomed by London high society, and enjoyed dancing with adoring admirers. Emma, handicapped by lameness, was unable to dance, but still enjoyed horse riding until nearly thrown by a horse.

When his sisters, Mary and Kate, moved to live nearer Hardy, Emma never visited them, ashamed of their Dorset accents, and Henry's rough appearance.

While still friendly with Florence Henniker, Hardy met a new love, Agnes Grove, the attractive daughter of General Pitt Rivers and was quickly enamoured of her. Agnes visited Maxgate several times, and when Emma, suffering from neuralgia or shingles and unwell, she acted as hostess for Hardy. Another lady interested in writing, Hardy was soon referring to her as 'my journalistic trainee,' and 'my good little pupil.'

Despite his pleasure at his new loves, Hardy still had periods of depression, suffering from rheumatic pains, and sadness after the death of his father, In one of his sad poems, he even wrote that it would have been better if he had died.

A few holidays in Brighton, the Midlands and also in Switzerland, seemed to bring them closer together for a while. They enjoyed the new craze of cycling, and often rode down the Dorset lanes together, but tension was soon there again.

In 1897 Emma found a new friend in a Cambridge Don, Mr. Pretor, to whom she poured out her troubles, and who, also knowing Hardy, tried, tactfully, to advise her that she should be proud to be married to one so famous.

When WESSEX POEMS was published in 1898, Emma was hurt again by Hardy's reminiscences of young and attractive women he had known, and that there was only one reference to their days of courtship in St. Juliot. She even felt that some of the poems were a direct attack on her.

When Rebekah and her sister left America to live permanently in the Lake District, although Rebekah was a worshipper at the shrine of Hardy, she also maintained friendly relations with Emma, between whom there was a considerable amount of friendly correspondence. But criticism of Hardy often appeared in Emma's letters, and in one of them, referring to his latest poems, she wrote 'I hope you don't like all his poems ... he should be the last man to disparage marriage. I have been a devoted wife for 20 years or more.' Her eyesight was poor; she had been forbidden to enter Hardy's study and she felt sure he had no love for her, but Hardy, too, was often hurt feeling that Emma no longer cared for him.

For his birthday, Emma bought him a Bible, always trying to change his agnosticism to more religious beliefs. Not surprisingly the Bible was put on one side. For her own birthday, she received a book from Mr. Pretor, with a dedication to her – Hardy did not even remember the date.

Their affection and friendship for the young Giffords continued, and Gordon was sent by Hardy to Paris to complete his education, while Emma taught him to paint. But not believing that women should have a career, Emma trained Lilian in house management and domestic matters only. Lilian became imbued with her Aunt's attitude of superiority, but also developed a spiteful nature as well.

About 1900 Emma went to Lee-on Solent to care for her sister, Helen, then ill, a widow, and living in Lee, and who died in October that year. Lilian was left in charge at Maxgate. While Emma was away there was a further visit from Rebekah whose obvious admiration for the great writer was much appreciated by Hardy – the three often enjoyed cycling together.

By 1901, there were more problems for Emma, who suffered greatly over the loss of her sister and also a feeling of general lassitude. She became more distressed by Hardy's lack of Christian feelings. She still agreed to go with him to London for their annual visit, but was tired and happy to return. At Maxgate she found more energy, and even managed to enjoy their usual garden parties, and the many visitors who came to Maxgate. Dorchester people still considered them a rather queer couple, and particularly Emma, who in her religious fervour insisted on giving religious tracts to as many people as possible, while she careered round the main streets of Dorchester on her green cycle, wearing bright green velvet.

Visitors to Maxgate were expected to be aware of Emma's good breeding and background and to admire her verses; she was most annoyed if she was ignored while her husband was praised.

In 1900 Hardy published another book of poems, again with a section on his earlier love affairs, causing more pain to his wife. He was also busy writing THE DYNASTS, an epic-drama in three parts, covering the Napoleonic period from 1805–15, but he often felt depressed and that he might not live to finish the work; often he was assailed by morbid feelings and thought often of death. He suffered from numerous colds and was troubled by his bladder problems, but he still carried on a lively correspondence with Florence Henniker and also Agnes Groves. He was grief-stricken when his dear Mother died in 1904 and again felt that his wife no longer cared for him. In 1901 their three cats were killed on the railway, and the fourth died shortly afterwards, adding to Emma's depression.

She found the annual London season worrying, and confessed that she was frightened to cross the busy London streets. She could still treat Hardy unkindly on occasions, as when they were invited to a garden party at Windsor Castle, on a hot day. There were insufficient seats in the carriage, and Emma's companion, noticing how frail Hardy was, offered him her seat, but Emma immediately and emphatically refused to allow this, saying that the walk would do him good, causing him to climb the hill and arrive perspiring and tired out.

To his dear friend Florence Henniker, Hardy would pour out his troubles, his depression and his sick headaches. Even after a successful dramatisation of TESS in London, he felt so miserable that he told her he would not be sorry to leave this world. Some of his friends thought his unfortunate marriage contributed to his depression. Emma too, unhappy, wrote to her friends of her troubles, particularly to Lady Hoare of Stourhead stating that her husband's books had not the same kind of interest for her as for others as she knew every word of his first editions from his manuscripts, that she was unhappy in Dorchester and had always hoped they would live in London; that she had been forbidden by Hardy to enter his study and only dared to enter when he was away from the house. Lady Hoare tried to be tactful in her reply. She was reading and enjoying many of Hardy's books and she referred to the fact that he was considered as our greatest literary giant.

By 1910 they had been estranged for several years. In the meantime Hardy had met his last great love, a young, delicate lady, with health problems, less than half his age, from a similar background as himself, a teacher, a writer of children's books, and the first woman to write for the defunct Daily Chronicle. He was immediately attracted to this young, gentle woman who he met in London about 1907. Her name was Florence Dugdale. Florence was happy to research for him, to type his manuscripts and to look up references for him for THE DYNASTS which he was then involved with. Soon they were enjoying holidays together in London and at Aldeburg, the home of his friend, Clodd.

How strange that a meeting at the Lyceum Club should result in the friendship for a time between the first Mrs. Hardy, who for some time knew nothing of her husband's latest affair, and the young lady who was destined to become the second Mrs. Hardy.

Emma was a strong supporter of the suffragist movement, and in 1907 actually marched with them in a parade in London. She was delighted to discover that Miss Dugdale also supported the movement, and more than pleased when she found out that Florence was also a writer – and a published one. Soon she was inviting her new friend to Maxgate. (Hardy, no doubt, was pleased with this arrangement; some suspect that he arranged the meeting at the Lyceum.)

Between 1910 and 1911 Florence visited Maxgate several times, on the invitation of her new friend, Emma, who was pleased to be able to show some of her unpublished efforts, particularly THE ACCEPTORS, a religious work, and her 35 year old manuscript, The MAID ON THE SHORE. When Florence was requested to retype and submit some of Emma's scripts to her own and other publishers, she willingly accepted. Florence's letters were always most encouraging, although she tried to be diplomatic by suggesting that some alterations needed to be made as to style and dress to update THE MAID ON THE SHORE.

Hardy was in London during Florence's first visit to Maxgate. On her return to London, and at Emma's request, she visited Hardy who was feeling tired and depressed. Rather hypocritically Hardy wrote to Emma ... "Miss Dugdale is coming this afternoon or to-morrow to see that I am alright. to put things straight ... and to type some letters for me."

To Mrs. Hardy, Florence wrote expressing sympathy for Emma's ill-health and saying, "I will with pleasure call at Mr. Hardy's flat as often as I can ... the anxiety as to how he is cannot be good for you. You will need all your strength for the great campaign which lies before us."

Emma was again writing poetry again, encouraged by Florence who was busy typing an article of her own before retyping MAID ON THE SHORE. Florence's efforts were not successful, but Emma's interest in writing was revived. It seems sad that Hardy who willingly helped so many writing 'friends' never assisted or encouraged his wife.

Florence was soon aware of the strained relationship at Maxgate and found herself in a difficult situation. At first her sympathies were with Emma, but this did not prevent the friendship with Hardy continuing. In his letters to his friend, Edward Clodd, Hardy often referred to Florence as 'my young friend' and 'my secretary,' He also wrote to Florence Henniker expressing his pleasure that the 'new' Florence had been to stay with her and that both ladies had enjoyed each other's company.

The strange, almost farcical relationship continued as Wife No. 1 entertained the young lady who was to succeed her. Florence even interviewed some prospective cooks for Emma, and also remembered Emma's birthday when no one else did, and listened attentively to both Hardy's and Emma's account of their unhappiness with each other.

In Nov. 1910 Florence wrote to Edward Clodd that Mrs. Hardy had become stranger than ever. Emma had suddenly asked her if she had noticed the likeness between Dr. Crippen, the wife murdered, and Hardy, and even wondered if she might be found mutilated in the cellar. Florence hastily departed at this stage in case Emma also thought she was like Miss Le Neve, Crippen's mistress.

Emma eventually realised that there was a strong bond of friendship between her husband and Florence. Not unnaturally she was both hurt and jealous, and retreated in annoyance to her boudoir attic rooms. Hardy was even using a separate staircase to avoid any meetings. They were said to be hardly on speaking terms with Hardy taking most of his meals in his study. Despite their differences their annual visit to London was spent together. On their return, although Emma was not feeling well, they held one of their large, popular garden parties at Maxgate. Shortly afterwards, Emma played her favourite tunes and finished by saying this would be the last time she would play any of them again.

One day Emma entered the forbidden studio and seeing the untidy table covered with remnants of his last meal, she spoke out and criticised the confused muddle when angry words arose between them which, later, he felt hastened Emma's final illness. Even towards the end Emma tried to arose Hardy's interest in her. She arranged for a pamphlet of her poems based on memories to be published by Longman's, Dorchester, to show him that they shared common interests in poetry. A growing shyness and restraint, a lack of conversation prevented a deeper contact. Her activities had become less and instead of racing through the lanes on her bicycle she usually attended Fordington church in a bath chair.

A young girl, Dolly Gale, was engaged in 1911 to be Emma's personal maid, Her sympathies were entirely with her mistress, and years later she was to describe Hardy as miserable, that they had little to do with each other and that there was hardly any conversation between them.

Between 1911 and 1912. Hardy was often away from Maxgate, either with relatives, or to London to meet Florence, and also to other areas. When at Maxgate he spent most of his time in his study composing poems or correcting proofs.

An unannounced visit from Rebekah and Catherine came at a time when Emma was suffering from back pains and debility, but she made an effort to entertain them, even persuading Hardy to come and talk to them, as it was he they really wanted to see. The sister realised that Emma was far from well, and tried to persuade her to see a doctor. Reluctantly she agreed to see Dr. Gowring, but refused to be examined by him. Both Emma and Hardy had a horror of operations. The doctor diagnosed weakness from lack of nourishment.

But the following day she was much worse, and sent the maid to Hardy's study to ask him to come to see her. Emma was practically unconscious when he reached her room. Dr. Gowring was sent for again, but it was too late and Emma was dead. The cause of death was then given as heart failure and gall-stones. Hardy was overcome with grief, and began to realise his neglect of her had resulted in his unawareness of her deteriorating health. In a letter to Florence Henniker he wrote, "I have reproached myself for not having guessed there might be some internal mischief at work, instead of blindly supposing her robust and sound and likely to live to quite an old age."

Hardy, lost, required help in Maxgate. The housekeeper, Florence Griffin, could manage the affairs of the house. A telegram was sent to Florence Dugdale, while Lilian Gifford arrived quickly.

Emma was buried in Stinsford churchyard on 30th Nov. 1912. The card with Hardy's wreath read 'From her lonely husband – with the old affection'. Denys

Kay-Robinson believed he could have added 'twenty years too late.'

The death of Emma seemed to revive happy memories of his earlier love for her. Words that he had failed to speak to her were expressed in moving poetry as his mind and thoughts reverted to a past which began in Cornwall. In his study, despite regret at his neglect, he was, in a sense, happy, as words and more words of a past that had vanished, and a love that had been lost, produced some of his finest poems.

Hardy's Cottage

FLORENCE DUGDALE

– THE SECOND MRS. THOMAS HARDY

Florence & Thomas Hardy

Helpless, sorrowful and alone, Hardy sent a telegram to Florence who was on her way to Weymouth to see a performance of THE TRUMPET MAJOR and to enjoy some of the healthful benefits of the sea air. In less than a month after Emma's death, she was at Maxgate. Hardy's household requirements were attended to by the housekeeper, Florence Griffin. Soon his niece, Lilian Gifford arrived. The little town of Dorchester was rife with rumours. Who would he marry next? It was already known in Dorchester that he had a mistress in London, thought to be Florence Dugdale.

When Hardy met Florence about 1907, he fell deeply in love with her, inscribing several of his books to her, contacting his publishers on her behalf and even putting her name to pieces he had written. His profound love for this young lady, half his age, was returned by Florence, who was equally attracted to the famous author. She delighted in being his research assistant, and even obtained a flat in London where they could be together. Often with Florence's poor health in mind, he was happy to take her on holiday to Ventnor, Aldeburgh (the home of his close friend, Edward Clodd) and to other places.

Prior to her friendship with Hardy, Florence had had a close relationship with another elderly gentleman, Sir William Thornley Stoker, a famous surgeon and a Governor of Dublin National Gallery. Several times she had stayed at his beautiful home, Ely House, Dublin, but there were problems. Like Rochester in 'Jane Eyre' he, too, had a mad wife. When he died in the summer of 1912, he left Florence £2,000 (a considerable sum then) and about one-sixth of the residue of his estate. Generously she paid for her sister, Marjorie, to attend a Domestic Science college for three years. In Hardy she saw another cultured, clever and famous person, but he, too, had a wife.

Trouble soon arose in the 'menage à trois' by Lilian asserting that it was her aunt's influence that had made Hardy a famous writer, and when Gordon, the nephew arrived, she was more than shocked when he informed Florence that his aunt had assured him that Maxgate would come to him after Hardy's death.

Florence Griffin, the housekeeper, was soon sent away by the other Florence, but her life at Maxgate was difficult and full of problems. She was conscious of the gossip concerning herself. If she walked in the streets of Dorchester with Hardy, or even without him, there was much gossiping. By Lilian, she had been reminded more than once, that her aunt was a very great lady, but the worst suffering came from the change in Hardy himself. Before the death of Emma, his concern was for his newly found love, and was particularly solicitous on account of her weak health. He was determined to help her in every way he could and especially to become a better known published writer.

After the death of Emma, and to the hurting surprise of Florence, he became aware of his neglect of Emma. To atone for past failings, to overcome a guilt complex and to show his remorse, his thoughts turned inward and to the past. Hours were spent in his study writing poetry about his lost love. He recalled the happy days in Cornwall, of their courtship and their attraction and affection for each other, forgetting that during Emma's life there were long periods of estrangement, bitterness and even, sometimes, hatred. As Irene Cooper Willis, one of his trustees, said 'It was bitter that Thomas Hardy should have fallen in love with Emma again as soon as she died, whereas while she was alive he could hardly bear to be near her.'

To Florence, this unexpected change seemed almost incredible. To make matters worse, she was expected to type and read aloud many of these romantic poems of a past which had been forgotten but which had reappeared. Not only was Florence expected to be concerned with the poems to his 'late espoused saint' as she bitterly referred to Emma, but was even expected sometimes to accompany

Hardy on pilgrimages to Plymouth (where he would never take Emma), Cornwall and St. Juliot and other places which had a romantic reminder of their courtship days.

With delight Hardy read Emma's RECOLLECTIONS of her life in Plymouth and her happiness in meeting him at St. Juliot. With feelings of horror and a morbid fascination he read over and over again Emma's BLACK DIARY of abuse and hate, with its heading WHAT I THINK OF MY HUSBAND, which were started in the 1890s and were continued practically up to her death. In his veneration of his past love, Hardy explained the diaries by a strangeness which had overcome Emma, and her strong religious views, almost a mania with her. Eventually he burned them. Over 50 poems were written during the two years after her death, which have been described as some of his greatest poetry.

In 'GOING' he wrote: 'Why, then, latterly did we not speak
Did we not think of those days long dead,
And ere your vanishing strive to seek,
That time's renewal?

Florence was again hurt as his poems showed a love for the dead wife which had not existed for many years. Sometimes he departed alone, or with his brother, Henry, leaving Florence by herself in the gloomy, isolated house. Not only was Florence unhappy, but she was frightened as well, and kept a loaded revolver in her room. Luckily she had the friendship of Hardy's sisters and brother who tried to help and comfort her. "As long as he does not meet another Gifford, all will be well." Their dislike of Emma was fixed and strong.

Florence was by then 35. In her loneliness and humiliation she felt totally compromised, and that no one would want to marry her. To overcome loneliness and fear she bought a rough-haired terrier, WESSEX, who became well known as a pampered dog whose bite was worse than his bark and who respected very few of the visitors to Maxgate.

Hardy's attitude to Florence had completely changed, and she felt he wanted a housekeeper who could also be a companion and help with his manuscripts. When Lilian arrived again with the idea of managing Maxgate and taking her aunt's place, Florence wrote to Edward Clodd in January 1914, "If she stays I go to my home and stay there."

Despite all her forebodings and problems, Thomas Hardy and Florence Dugdale were married on February 13th 1914 quietly, at St. Andrews Parish Church, Enfield. She was given away by her father, Headmaster of Enfield Church School, and where Florence had taught also. Her youngest sister, Marjorie, and Hardy's brother, Henry, were at the wedding.

To Sir Sidney Cockerell, the Director of Fitzwilliam Museum at Cambridge and a Literary Executor of Hardy's will, she explained that she married Hardy to express her devotion and to endeavour to add to his comfort and happiness. She felt that she could not have stayed indefinitely at Maxgate if she had not married him.

After the wedding Florence began to feel better and more sure of herself. She looked forward to meeting more of Hardy's friends. To provide more comfort for guests she had a bedroom enlarged, and to avoid being in the house when workmen were busy and making a noise, they went to Cambridge when she enjoyed being Mrs. Hardy and meeting some of his friends.

On 4th August 1914 they had to face the horror of the country at war. Hardy was terrified in case Germans should arrive on the Dorset coast and could not bear Florence to be away from him even though he spent long periods in his study.

In a new collection of poems, SATIRES OF CIRCUMSTANCES there were many intimate poems but very few about Florence.Florence was also dismayed by the sadness of some of the poems and felt sometimes that all he wanted was to be in his grave next to Emma. His feelings were expressed in THE VOICE and in other poems:

> Woman much missed, how you call to me, call to me
> Saying that now you are not as you were
> When you had changed from the one who was all to me
> But as at first, when our day was fair.

Florence's health problems increased, but Hardy did not want her to leave him for treatment. When a nasal operation became imperative she had to go to a London Nursing Home for treatment, but Hardy did not even visit her and, it was said that he did not pay the nursing fees.

As he grew older, he became 'tight' with money although he was reputed to be the richest author in England. He refused to give Florence a settlement on marriage, but gave her a very small housekeeping allowance which often proved inadequate. About this time the family became concerned that his money should go to a genuine member of the Hardy family and not to Florence or her side.

Hurt that his previous tenderness and concern for her delicate health, seemed to belong to the past, she sometimes thought that he no longer cared for her and in her bitterness declared that if her name had been GIFFORD he would have looked after her more and taken her on holidays as before they were married. Although he readily accepted hospitality from others, he showed no wish to return it, becoming more and more a recluse.

Florence agreed that a 'Hardy' born should succeed to Maxgate and some of the possessions and also with the choice of a cousin Frank George Hardy. To their dismay he was killed in battle in August 1915. A few months later Hardy's beloved sister, Mary died, who had always been very close to him. His thoughts went further and further to the past, spending hours in his studio where he could conveniently shut out the present. Florence, not being able to participate in this passion for the past, felt life was difficult and grim. They were both upset when they heard that their friend, Clodd, was to publish his reminiscences, because of their visits to Aldeburg before the death of Emma. On the spur of the minute Florence wrote an angry letter to him. At this time her opinions of others seemed to change. Cockerell, whom she originally liked, she now disliked, and this included others, both friends and relations.

Further illness and nose and ear infection necessitated further treatment. Even then her only means of having a healthful holiday was to agree to visit Launceston to visit members of the Gifford family and to St. Juliot's to see the memorial to Emma that he had designed and paid for.

There were also troubles with Florence's own family, mostly due to illness and lack of money. Sadly she wrote, "Sometimes I feel 80," but Hardy remained well and cheerful. To Rebekah Owen she wrote, 'Strangers must imagine that his only wish is to die and be in the grave with the only woman who gave him happiness.'

By 1916 Florence was still reviewing books for London editors, besides managing the house, acting as Hardy's secretary; she also looked after the garden and even purchased a flock of Rhode Island Red hens, while Hardy commented in a letter to Florence Henniker on their quiet and uneventful lives.

The following year Florence complained that her secretarial duties were causing eye strain, but Hardy was still thinking of the dead Emma. Friends sympathized with her over the wraith of Emma which lingered in the house. In her diary she wrote that on each anniversary of Emma's death he went into mourning. 'It is very pathetic when one remembers what his married life was like.' However unhappy she was Florence continued to give devotion and care of her husband. Friends as T.E. Lawrence and Sir James Barry realised her problems and praised her for her devotion to her husband. To Cockerell she wrote that she felt she had 'gone from youth to dismal old age.' Although Hardy's world was immersed in the past, perhaps he began to realise some of the hurt experienced by Florence. He inscribed the first copy of his verses MOMENTS OF VISION 'The first copy of the first edition to the first of women, Florence Hardy'. But everything at Maxgate had to remain as it was in Emma's days. The garden had to stay the same and Florence was not allowed to move the position of any of the furniture.

Frequent requests for a Hardy biography or an autobiography gave rise to problems owing to his hidden meetings with Florence during the lifetime of Emma. Also as Hardy became more famous he hid or minimised his early peasant background. They both were concerned that if someone else wrote the book, there was no knowing what revealing items might be mentioned. After much discussion and thought, they found a solution – to write it himself, but to be inscribed under the name of Florence and to be published after his death,as a biography by Florence. It was to be written in the third person. Texts, diaries, original documents were incorporated and were typed by Florence, after which most of them were destroyed. Fortunately for Florence, Hardy's love letters to Emma and her replies had been burned by Emma, although sections of Emma's SOME RECOLLECTIONS were included. Florence still suffered much as reminders of visits with Emma were discussed, sometimes to places where he had taken Emma, but refused to take Florence. Emphasis was laid on the fact of how unexpected the death of Emma was to him, and their regret that they had no child – all very hurtful to Florence. Besides this she was responsible for answering Hardy's ever increasing volume of correspondence.

On his 80th birthday, there were over 200 telegrams of congratulation to be answered by Florence, as well as the organisation of the house. By August 1920, Florence had, at long last, managed to persuade Hardy to have a bathroom installed instead of the inconvenience of pumping water from the well and then heating it. That year he was also made Hon. D. Lit of Oxford. After the war there were admiring visits from many well known writers, as Siegfried Sassoon, Walter De La Mare, Galsworthy, T.E. Lawrence, Sir James Barry, and Florence blossomed in their company and slowly lost some of her early fears. Work continued on an enormous scale.

In February 1924, Florence was appointed as a Magistrate of the Borough; her husband was already a County Magistrate. They were both distinguished members of the Dorset Debating and Dramatic Society, often acting as judges for some events. Florence also became a member of the Board of Governors of the County School for Girls, at Dorchester, and an active member of other local committees. Occasionally she managed to escape from the rather grim atmosphere of Maxgate, to friends in London when she was delighted to be taken on shopping expeditions and to the theatre – and also managed to get a telephone installed in Maxgate.

As Hardy grew older he became more active, while Florence suffered more from health problems, and in 1924 an operation for the removal of a gland from her neck became essential, and from which she returned looking elderly and worn, although still only 45.

Hardy was upset, when, in 1923, Florence Henniker died, after 30 years of friendship. In that year also he was honoured by a visit from the Prince of Wales (Edward VIII) and at last local people began to be impressed by the fame of the writer in their midst, who was almost unique in the number of poems and lyrics he continued to write.

In 1926 there was more sadness when AGNES GROVE died and three weeks later their much beloved and petted dog, WESSEX died. The following year was the twelfth anniversary of the death of his dear sister, MARY HARDY, and the 15th anniversary of EMMA. Pathetically he wore an old black hat and carried Emma's walking stick.

He had become much weaker, but still enjoyed walks through his pleasant garden, assisted by Florence. In Dec. 1927, Florence wrote to Lady Hoare, "Thomas has been in bed for over three weeks and is very unwell . . . he is making a good fight . . . his mind is clear and vigorous, but his body is so frail. Florence's sister, Eva Dugdale, matron of a Masonic Hospital in London, stayed with him during his last few days and had the highest regard for his gentleness and consideration as a patient. At 9 p.m. on January 11th, he died.

His death brought wrangling. Sir Sydney Cockerell and Sir James Barry who were in the house, made arrangements for a funeral service at Westminster Abbey. But Florence, his sister, Kate, and other members of the family were unhappy, knowing that he had always expressed the wish to be buried at the little Stinsford Church by the side of Emma, his parents and other members of the family. Deeply upset, Florence consulted their local Vicar who suggested a compromise – his heart to be buried at Stinsford and his ashes in the Abbey. The family were disgusted, and in Dorchester crude remarks were passed around, 'ALMIGHTY, e'll say "Ere be 'eart, but where be rest of'e?'

The arguments continued, mainly with Cockerell, but Florence agreed with him on one important matter, that much of the correspondence relating to Hardy's past should be burnt. In November 1930 local subscription had arranged for a stained glass memorial window to be erected at Stinsford. Florence was asked to unveil it, but as Somerset Maugham had just published his book, CAKES & ALE about the second wife of a famous man taking advantage of his position, always sensitive, Florence thought it was directed at her, and refused.

Florence was 49 when Hardy died and the rest of her life was mainly sad, although she was able to buy a car, new furniture and visit the continent.

The LIFE OF HARDY was produced in November, the year of Hardy's death, when Florence removed all complimentary references to Emma, followed in 1930 by THE LATER YEARS. The book received criticism for its 'odd' approach, while discerners soon realised that these were the works of an older man, whose stilted language showed that it was the work of a person who had not written prose for very many years.

Florence maintained a friendship with many well known people, and it was even thought at one time that she could have married either Siegfried Sassoon or Sir James Barry, but she remained Mrs. Thomas Hardy, always being proud of his name.

She died on 17th October 1937 of cancer and was buried at Stinsford.

LADY WIMBORNE OF CANFORD

Through the development of pig iron in South Wales, John Guest and other members of the family became rich and influential, not only in business, but in politics and religious matters. Kindly John Guest also tried to alleviate the dreadful conditions of poverty and suffering then existing in Merthyr Tydfil. For his efforts for the town he was elected as Liberal candidate for Merthyr in 1832, and became the first of many Guests to enter parliament, and in 1838 John was knighted, becoming Sir John.

A new House had been purchased in Canford, Dorset, and by 1851, Sir John was spending more time there than in Wales. On his death, his eldest son, Sir Ivor Guest became Lord Wimborne. In 1868 he married Cornelia Henrietta Maria Spencer Churchill, born in 1847, the eldest daughter of the 7th Duke of Marlborough and sister to Randolph Churchill. Cornelia was vivacious, beautiful, petite and also strong-willed. She was described as the 'real dynamo' at Canford Manor – charming, but when opposed could show her temper. She was an eloquent speaker and expressed herself forcibly when explaining many of her sound ideas. She was a strong advocate of temperance and a staunch supporter of the Church of England to whom she donated large sums of money. Liberally minded in many ways, she also donated money for the upkeep of non-conformist chapels and churches.

Although she had nine children, she still found time to help the poor in the area and was always willing to listen to their problems. She was involved with many of her husband's affairs who was also a caring person and a good organiser. They also entertained well and many members of royal families and nobility were welcomed at the Manor.

In 1871 they bought a fine house, 22 Arlington Street, London, which they renamed Wimborne House and where they could take part in the high society, social life of those times. Lord Wimborne would also be able to become more involved in political matters.

Many lavish banquets were held there, when there was usually dancing in the magnificent ballroom to the small hours. The house remained in the ownership of members of the Guest family until 1947 when it was sold and purchased by an Insurance Company.

At Canford, in 1873, there were special celebrations in honour of the birth of the fourth child, a son and heir, named Ivor Churchill. An enormous fête was held for 183,500 tenants and 1,400 cottagers. There was dancing and fireworks with the name of the new heir in the centre of a spectacular display.

In 1880 Sir Ivor became Baron Lord Wimborne, with a seat in the House of Lords.

At Branksome Dene, their summer residence by the sea, many of the Guest family enjoyed delightful holidays there and enjoyed the lavish entertainments, including Thomas Hardy and his first wife, Emma. Lord Randolph Churchill and his family often came to Branksome Dene. It was there that the young Winston Churchill nearly lost his life. Trying to avoid capture by his younger brother and cousin, he leapt into the top of a fir tree and crashed to the ground 29 feet below. He was unconscious for three days after this escapade. Branksome Dene was sold by Lord Wimborne at the beginning of the 20th century. At one time it was owned by Sir Ernest Cassells, millionaire grandfather of Edwina Mountbatten. Today, as Zetland Court, it is a residential home of the Masonic Benevolent Society.

In 1885 a new parliamentary constituency was formed for East Dorset, when a great political rally was held at Canford Manor. Lord Wimborne, had, by then, transferred to the Conservative Party and Lady Wimborne had become a strong supporter of the Primrose League, a branch of the Conservative Party to honour the memory of Disraeli who was very fond of primroses. There were over 50,000 people in Canford Park and thousands more lining the route of the huge procession. Visitors at the Manor included the Dowager Duchess of Marlborough, Lady Sarah Churchill, Lord and Lady Randolph Churchill and many others, all greeted by Lord and Lady Wimborne.

Nearby Broadstone owed much of its development to the Wimbornes, Lord Wimborne was responsible for the opening of a school in 1871 when Lady Wimborne became a frequent visitor and expected a high standard in needlework and other subjects. When Lord Wimborne laid out a golf course there, his wife had a shelter constructed to encourage the ladies to play also.

When a Park for the benefit of the people of Poole was discussed, Lord Wimborne readily donated 26 acres of land for the project. As the Prince of Wales (Edward VII) and Prince George were visiting Canford Manor at that time, they were delighted to open the new park on 17th January 1890. A large pavilion was erected in the park for the ceremony. Owing to a flu epidemic, Lord Wimborne was unable to attend, but his two sons, Ivor and Montagu Guest welcomed the Prince and his entourage. There was a reception in Bournemouth at the Royal Bath Hotel with decorations and bunting everywhere and more receptions at Canford in honour of their royal guests. Lady Wimborne, as usual, had been closely involved with the royal arrangements for the 'park for the people', which, today, is visited and enjoyed by thousands of visitors.

There was also the official opening of the Royal Victoria Hospital, Poole Road, a splendid memorial to Queen Victoria's Golden Jubilee. Lady Wimborne, who was greatly interested in the development of hospitals and the care of the sick, was present at the opening. In 1889, Lady Wimborne purchased a house in West Street, Poole, which became the Cornelia Cottage Hospital with fourteen beds and a convalescent wing. This was later transferred to Weston House where there was more accommodation (now demolished) and where a laundry was started to give employment to young girls and to give service to the hospital. Moved to better premises again, in Market Street, it was still known as the Cornelia Hospital. When there was a deficiency in the accounts, Lady Wimborne made up the difference, also making up the difference when the Boscombe Hospital Bazaar's subscriptions were inadequate'

In 1899, Lady Wimborne, always trying to improve conditions, purchased the Red Star Coffee Tavern in Poole for a lodging house for seamen and encouraged classes to be commenced in horticulture at Canford Technical Committee.

In 1904 their political persuasion reverted to Liberalism again, when many Liberal Women's Associations were formed. Plots of land were sold from the Canford Estate at incredibly cheap prices, between £4 and £8, while gas, water, electricity would be laid on. In Newtown, land was made available for working men on easy terms. As the result of a visit to Hampstead Garden City in 1909, Lady Wimborne explained the advantages of the system of co-partnership.

By about 1906 Lord Wimborne's health had deteriorated and from that time Lady Wimborne practically managed the estate showing her business qualities as well as those of caring for the less well-off. She was becoming more and more interested in the development of allotments and horticulture, and sent a group of farmers and others to investigate smallholdings and rearing poultry in Denmark, after which she published a pamphlet entitled, 'Some Impressions of Danish Methods of Agriculture.' In her opinion, Britain was considerably behind the rest of the world in agricultural development, and to encourage matters she allotted 54 acres of land for smallholdings near Alder Road, at £50 per acre on easy terms. In 1909 the Borough Allotments Association of Poole was commenced by Lady Wimborne who further explained the advantages of purchasing seeds and marketing their goods co-operatively. To show what could be achieved she arranged for a 4 acre French garden to be developed at Stanley Green, Poole, to test intensive cultivation under cloches, as she had seen in France. Many meetings were held on smallholdings, housing and development of education. At Canford there were spectacular horse raising events, but care of the tenants was also important. Farm rents were raised when conditions were good and lowered when they were poor.

Besides the many festivities at Canford, many meetings and discussions were held, when Lady Wimborne presided or other members of the Guest family. The family were interested in all aspects of bettering conditions and development in Poole. Liberal Sports Committees were formed, there was the Cornelia Football Club in Poole and a Cornelia Girls' Club. Working Men's Clubs were formed and land was given for the opening of schools.

To safeguard the treasures at Canford, Lady Wimborne actually purchased a fire engine and raised a part-time force of 18 men, who would also assist in fighting forest fires and other disasters in the area. By her example and encouragement to others, Lady Wimborne showed what women could achieve, helping to raise the status of women in a mostly male dominated society.

In 1911 she was asked to allow the artist Augustus John to become a tenant at Alderney Manor. Although he had an unsavoury reputation, she was interested in all aspects of art, and was pleased to welcome him, and was never disturbed when she saw his several naked children running around the Manor grounds. Augustus John enjoyed the company of gypsies, and the tolerant Cornelia encouraged them to live at Canford Heath. (Alderney Manor was demolished for housing, after the death of Lady Wimborne in 1927).

Lord Wimborne died in 1914. His widow stayed at Canford until 1922 when the House was sold and became Canford School. Lady Canford moved to Merley House, another Guest property and died in 1927. Both were buried at Canford Church.

In October 1906 Lady Wimborne laid the corner stone for a new hospital on land provided from the Canford Estate – in Longfleet Road (then Ringwood Road). The new Cornelia Hospital was opened by Lady Wimborne on 3rd May 1907, having cost £3,369!

During the First World War, Lady Wimborne was always an active worker. Soldiers were billeted at Canford Manor, while German prisoners of war worked in the grounds. This most active lady also founded the Dorset Guild of Workers whose members sent parcels to British prisoners of war. Cornelia Hospital was demolished in the 1960's when the present Poole General Hospital was constructed on the site and was opened by Queen Elizabeth II in 1969. Today there stands an enormous Cornelia Nurses Home and, close by, Cornelia House, a lecture room for training nurses. From small beginnings by a great and devoted lady this mighty hospital of today has a fine reputation as a caring and up-to-date modern hospital with the latest technological equipment.

There was a good family relationship among the Guests and Lady Wimborne was always interested in their careers. She was especially fond of her brother, Randolph Churchill, and also of his son, (her grandson) Winston Churchill, and keenly followed his career. It was said that Winston made his first political speech on the lawns at Canford Manor, and when he was elected for Oldham and made his first maiden speech in 1901, his grandmother, Lady Wimborne, was there, proud and happy to give him her moral support. When Winston decided to write the biography of his father, Lady Wimborne, devoted to her brother, was happy and able to pass to Winston material and scrapbooks she had kept on the life of Lord Randolph. For many years Lady Wimborne had been considered one of the most influential women in the political world and together with other members of the family played an important part in the help given to Winston both politically and in many other ways.

Although Lady Wimborne has been described as autocratic as she became more elderly, Poole and area owe a great deal to the generosity and interest in local affairs of the Wimbornes and their family. Their memories are honoured in many ways throughout Poole and area and also in Canford Manor, again made famous by the success and abilities of the students at this outstanding Public School.

Canford School, formerly Canford Manor

LILLIE LANGTRY

and her BOURNEMOUTH CONNECTION

So many books and plays have been written about the celebrated beauty, Lillie Langtry, who took London by storm during the 19th century, about this amazing personality with her magnetic charm and will continue to be written.Lillie came from a simple and religious background, in the quiet and rather puritanical Channel Islands of that time. Those who knew her as a child never imagined that one day she would become famous, the sensation of London and known throughout the world. Crowds clambered on chairs and pushed against each other to get a better view of her when she rode on horseback in Rotten Row while guests gasped in astonishment at her wondrous beauty when she entered a room.

Lillie became the first publicly acknowledged, official mistress of the Prince of Wales who became Edward VII, while remaining on friendly terms with his lovely wife, Princess Alexandra, She was even presented at Court before Queen Victoria.

John Everett Millais, who also originated from the Channel Islands said "Lillie Langtry happens to be the most beautiful woman on earth" while George Bernard Shaw commented, "She has no right to be intelligent, daring and independent, as well as lovely – a frightening combination of attributes," but the most ecstatic praise came from the very attractive, younger lady, who succeeded her in 1889 as the Prince's next official mistress, Daisy Countess of Warwick: "How can any words of mine convey her beauty? She had dewy, violet eyes, a complexion like a peach and a mass of lovely hair drawn back in a soft knot . . . Her vitality, the glow and amazing charm made this fascinating woman the centre of any group she entered."

But what of the Bournemouth connection? The town is unable to boast of many historic buildings, several having disappeared under the hammer of the demolition man. But the Langtry Manor Hotel, a listed building, originally known as The Red House, because of its red bricks and red-tiled roof, was the home of Lillie for over four years, from 1879. It became known as her love-nest, and was constructed on behalf of her royal lover.

Lillie was born in Jersey in the Channel Islands on Oct. 13th, 1853, the only girl among six lively brothers. It is not surprising that she became a tom-boy and willingly took part in their pranks. Her father became known as the randy Dean of Jersey, because of his several 'affairs' with local women. Her mother, an ambitious woman, had great ideas for Lillie's future, preferably on the mainland, ideas shared by Lillie herself.

Tired of the restricted life in the Channel Islands, she was pleased to marry Edward Langtry in March 1874, a supposedly wealthy, idle widower and the owner of a superb 80 foot yacht, the Red Gauntlet. Her aim was to get away from the Island and to find fame and fortune on the mainland, preferably in London. Later she was to confess that it was the yacht, with its crew of five, and not the owner, which attracted her.

Life in Southampton with Edward gave her little satisfaction, but a move to Eaton Place, London, was more to her taste. Then she felt she was really among the aristocracy with Dukes and Earls as neighbours. At last they were in the great metropolis where famous artists, actors, the élite of society, and particularly the Prince and Princess of Wales, were to be seen.

In London she eventually met Lord Ranelagh, a former Channel Islander, who invited herself and her husband to one of his receptions. This marked the beginning of her entrance into society. People (men particularly) were charmed by her exquisite features, her purity of expression, her calmness and deep violet eyes. In her simple tight fitting black dress (she was in mourning for the death of her youngest brother) which stood out among the elaborate and stylish gowns seen at the reception the male guests were attracted to her as moths to a bright

47

flame. Invitations poured on them from the high society world, delighting Lillie and displeasing her husband who was practically ignored. She was introduced to Millais, who was enchanted by her beauty, and asked her to sit for a portrait. Lord Frederick Leighton, President of the Royal Academy, arranged to model a bust of her in marble, while Frank Miles, a young artist, quietly drew pen and ink sketches of her, one of which he gallantly presented to her. Reproduction of the others was made, and soon her amazing beauty had reached a wider public in the form of postcards in many shops sold at one penny (old money) each.

As the result of increasing publicity her face became one of the best known in London. It was not surprising that the Prince of Wales who had an eye for attractive women should become interested in the lovely Jersey Lily, as she became known.

An introduction was arranged; their attraction was mutual and Lillie had the honour of becoming his first mistress to be publicly acknowledged. She was invited to all the best houses. If a hostess wanted the Prince to be present, she knew that Lillie must be invited too. As for Edward Langtry, no one wanted to meet him. For consolation he started to drink heavily.

The Prince of Wales – Bertie, as he was known – completely charmed by the lovely Lillie broke one of his rules concerning mistresses, whom he usually rewarded with a piece of jewellery. In 1877, shortly after they met, he ordered the building of a fine house for her in the newly developed watering place of Bournemouth among pine trees and with a good view of the sea, which meant so much to Lillie. There they could meet in peace and away from the crowded life of London society and gossip.

This was Lillie's house, built to her requirements, and provided by Edward. Like her royal lover she had a great disregard for conventionality, so it is not surprising to see the words 'THEY SAY, WHAT SAY THEY? LET THEM SAY' engraved on the Minstrels' Gallery. On a beam in the palatial entrance hall is the hospitable greeting, 'AND YOURS TOO, MY FRIENDS.'

Throughout the house, we can see evidence of the pride she had in her new home among the pines. For her royal admirer, her 'Bertie' she created a welcoming atmosphere everywhere. On an outside wall by Edward's bedroom is the Latin inscription STET FORTUNA DOMUS – May fortune attend those who dwell here – and on an exterior wall near Lillie's room, DULCE DOMUM – a sweet home. On a foundation stone, the date, 1877 and E.L.L. which stands for Emilie le Breton Langtry was engraved (Lillie's maiden name was Emilie le Breton, but because of her lily-white complexion and her difficulty in saying the word 'Emilie', she was always known as Lillie, or the Jersey Lily – after the painting by Millais.

The dining room is magnificent. You sense the presence of royalty, love, frivolity and happiness. You can imagine the highborn and their sumptuous meals, fêting the beautiful Lillie. High up in a corner, near the gallery, is a small hatchway which opened on the first floor, and from where Edward could inspect the guests before descending the staircase. Over the exquisitely carved mantelpiece in which the initials E.L.L. are again incorporated, is an original painting of Edward by Heywood Hardy, with his faithful hunting dog besides him. Nearby is a fine reproduction of a portrait of Lillie.

Throughout the building the atmosphere of romance is felt among the several portraits of Lillie and her Prince, including the three beautiful heads of Lillie sketched by Frank Miles. Lillie's love of romance is shown in the intertwining swans' necks in the colourful stained-glass window.

The building has been a hotel for many years. Until fairly recently many people were unaware that it had been the home of the lovely Lillie. A few years ago the present owners decided that they would like to restore the building to its original condition, but with today's amenities. Edward's bedroom had been made into three small rooms, and a lower, false ceiling put in the room. After many months of hard work, the original oak-beamed ceiling was revealed and also the original hand-painted murals which had been covered by layers of wallpaper. When the blocked-up fireplace was eventually uncovered, it was discovered that there were inglenooks and oak beams reaching up to the ceiling, but there was a further surprise in store. The surround had been mounted with 18 skilfully hand-painted tiles in blue, white and gold leaf which were as clean and fresh as they would have been when a fire was lit for the Prince of Wales. Each tile portrayed scenes from Shakespearean plays, all of which had been individually chosen by Lillie, showing her love of the theatre, from which later she acquired more fame as a celebrated actress and producer.

The restored fireplace in The Prince of
Wales's bedroom, Langtry Manor

A feature of Lillie's rooms are the extremely wide doorways, especially designed to give ample space for the fashionable gowns worn then. It was said that she took cold baths every morning, exercised and enjoyed long country walks. To preserve her complexion she went to bed with raw, minced beef on her face, not it is thought when Bertie was present.

With her diamond ring, she scratched on a ground floor window, the familiar E.L.L. AND TWO HEARTS pierced by an arrow, also the word 'Dora' said to be Edward's pet name for her, with the date 1883. On a second window the letters E.L.L. and N.L.L., (this latter is a mystery, no one being quite sure what was intended).

Lillie's residence in Bournemouth at the Red House (now the Langtry Manor Hotel) was a time of happiness, but also one of discretion. In the weekly lists of roads and inhabitants, her name appeared as 'Mrs. Langton and family'. She sometimes let the mansion if she was staying in London or abroad for long periods. In 1883. Oscar Wilde, one of her many admirers gave recitals at the Theatre Royal, in Albert Road, Bournemouth. As Lillie was also resident in Bournemouth that week, it is wondered whether he was invited to the Red House to stay there. That he was infatuated with her, there is no doubt, and even wrote a long poem dedicated to Lillie, entitled The New Helen – To Helen, formerly of Troy, now of London.

> Lily of love, pure and inviolate!
> Tower of ivory! Red rose of fire
> Thou has come down our darkness to illume . . .

The love affair between Bertie and herself lasted for about ten years, but even after she had been replaced in his affection by other mistresses, their friendship remained, and even after the death of King Edward in 1910, this was continued by his son, George V.

As the result of a further introduction some years later to Prince Louis Battenburg, a nephew of the Prince of Wales, they too became lovers, with the result that a child was born in great secrecy. Although living separately from Edward Langtry, who had become an alcoholic, he refused to allow her to divorce him. The baby daughter was named Jeanne Marie, and taught to call Lillie 'Ma Tante'. When she discovered that she was the illegitimate daughter of Lillie, she was horrified and never forgave her mother. Her daughter became Mary Malcolm and the first women presenter in television.

When Lillie became practically penniless, it was the Prince, by then her friend, who suggested that she went on the stage, becoming the first society lady to do so. Her name, her fame, her notoriety, guaranteed large audiences, attendances also helped by the support of the Prince and Princess of Wales.

Edward Langtry, often drunk, lonely and dissolute, died penniless in 1897. He had been financially maintained by Lillie for some years on condition that he made no attempt to contact her. Resolutely, to the end of his life, he refused her requests for a divorce. Now she was free!

In 1899 she met Hugo de Bathe, 19 years younger than Lillie, whom she married that year. After the death of his father, she was proud to become Lady de Bathe. At last she had achieved a real title. She continued to act and even had her own theatre, the Imperial, furnished with over 2,000 plush seats.

Lillie died in Monaco at Villa de Lys, in February 1929, at the age of 72, still beautiful and a celebrity.

How Lillie would have loved to stay at the Langtry Manor Hotel today. Her delightful bedroom with heart-shaped bath and magnificent four-poster bed, is well known as a 'honeymoon' suite, when young lovers have confessed that they felt a special atmosphere of love and romance in the room. Edwardian Banquets are a popular feature of the hotel, when a look-alike King Edward sometimes makes a regal appearance. Son et Lumière is also performed there through lights and music giving a little of the life of Lillie and her Prince in the days of the Red House. The portraits on the wall seem to look down approvingly.

Lillie's affection for her mansion by the sea was so strong that it is said that she reappears from time to time – a beautiful lady gliding through the rooms. She has been seen in the kitchen by the chef in the early hours of the morning, and also at 4 p.m., the time when she ordered afternoon tea. Sometimes a carriage has been seen outside with Lillie and the Prince inside it. Amidst the bright lights and happy gatherings at the Langtry Manor the love story of Lillie and her 'Bertie' will never die.

LADY RUSSELL-COTES and SIR MERTON

Benefactors of Bournemouth

The life, love and kindness of Annie Russell-Cotes is completely entwined with the same qualities in her husband. Both were benefactors to the town of Bournemouth, delighting in well-doing to the town which had become so important to them. Their life together for over 60 years was one of devotion and caring. Throughout his life Merton Russell-Cotes referred to her as his beloved wife and life-long companion.

Annie Russell-Cotes was born in Glasgow on 15th July 1835, the daughter of John King Clark, a kind and well thought of gentleman. She was educated in London where she studied music and singing. It was in Glasgow that Merton Russell-Cotes met his future wife. He was impressed with her magnificent contralto voice and her charm, so different from other girls he had met in Glasgow.

They were married on 1st February 1860, the beginning of a long period of great happiness for the two people.

For health reasons, the young man had been advised to travel abroad to warmer climates. Because of his great love of beautiful objets d'art, antiques, porcelain, paintings, wherever he went he collected curios and mementoes of his travels. After marriage he was accompanied by his beloved wife who shared his interest in fine and exquisite objects.

As a result of frequent attacks of bronchitis, he was advised to live permanently in the south of England, and 16 years later, they moved from Glasgow to Bournemouth, where he was persuaded to purchase the Bath Hotel. After discussions with his wife and other advisers, he became the owner of the hotel in 1876 and where he would be able to display his wonderful art treasures.

Extensions to the hotel were made, which was re-opened in August 1880 by Sir Francis Wyatt Truscott, Lord Mayor of London. Soon the hotel was resplendent with priceless paintings and treasures from many countries. Many famous and royal visitors came to the Royal Bath Hotel, as it became known, including Empress Eugenie, the Queen of Sweden, Edward VII, Prince Oscar of Sweden and his bride and many others. Merton became involved, almost immediately, in public affairs, always encouraged and helped by his wife.

In 1883 he was made a member of the Board of Commissioners, and together with Annie took a great interest in the development of the new town. Their benevolence, charity and good works commenced from their early days in Bournemouth and continued throughout their lives.

It was considered by Russell-Cotes and members of the medical profession that a hospital for infectious diseases was essential. But the idea of a fever hospital horrified people, and to his distress he received anonymous and abusive letters, while his effigy and that of members of the Board were publicly burnt. Talking the problem over with his wife, she suggested that Sanitary Hospital would be a more acceptable title, and a vexed question had been solved by his understanding wife. Due to the strain, Russell-Cotes became ill again and on the recommendation of his doctor friends went abroad again to rest and recover his health. On their return to Bournemouth two years later they were delighted to find that the Sanitary Hospital had been erected in Gloucester Road, Boscombe.

When Bournemouth became a Municipal Borough in 1890, Mr. and Mrs. Russell-Cotes were delighted. To show their pleasure they presented a mace and mayoral badge, the loop consisting of 18-carat gold, richly ornamented, with the motto PULCHRITUDO ET SALUBRITAS engraved on the badge.

In 1891 Russell-Cotes was invited to become Mayor, but as some members opposed his Undercliff Scheme, which he considered essential to prevent cliff erosion and a necessary addition to the amenities of the town, he refused. It was not until 1894 that the Council agreed to support his plans on condition that he accept an appointment as a magistrate in addition to that of Mayor. To celebrate this eventful period, and as a birthday present for his wife, Russell-Cotes commissioned the building of a magnificent hall on the East Cliff, facing the sea (Now the Russell-Cotes Art Gallery and Museum). The hall was erected in a style combining Italian Renaissance and Old Scottish Baronial.

After further delays the first section of the Undercliff was commenced in January 1907. To show his appreciation of this great achievement, he donated his fine art treasures to his adopted town, while his wife presented their home, East Cliff Hall as an Art Gallery and Museum, together with a fund for the maintenance of their memorabilia.

For their generosity and unceasing work for the betterment of Bournemouth, Mr. and Mrs. Russell-Cotes were made Honorary Freemen of the Borough in 1908 and in the following year a knighthood was bestowed on the worthy couple by King Edward VII.

In their many travels throughout the world, Lady Russell-Cotes was a constant and faithful companion. She was made a Fellow of the Royal Society of Literature after writing a book on their many travels. With her husband she explored the Sandwich Islands, including the great volcano Kilauea, actually going across the floor of the crater to the active lake of fire. In 1916, when she was 82, she gave additional money for an extension to the Gallery when she was presented with a beautifully framed, sealed copy of the Resolution thanking her for her kindness. The extension was opened by Princess Beatrice (the Princess Henry of Batten-berg). Unfortunately Lady Russell-Cotes was unwell and, to her great disappoint-ment, was unable to attend.

On the occasion of their Diamond Wedding in 1920, more gifts were donated to the town. These included £8,000 in connection with a Russell- Cotes Nautical Training College at Parkstone, land and £3,000 for the Shaftesbury Society for poor children. Lady Russell-Cotes also presented six houses to the Royal Victoria Hospital and £500 to Dr. Barnardos Home, besides other donations.

Her illness continued and in April 1920 this great and kind lady died and was buried in the family Mausoleum at Rush Corner (now Cemetery Junction). Her heartbroken husband wrote in his Autobiography

> "Dear wife beloved,
> Still in my heart thy face I'll keep,
> Still in mine eyes thy dear face,
> Until we meet again."

There were multitudes of flowers, letters and reports, all praising 'a lady whose life was made up of good works and who has left the impress of a gracious personality on the whole town.'

Sir Merton, missing the lady who had been everything to him, strove to carry on, but after a short illness died in January the following year, happy in a release which allowed him to join his dear wife again.

Memories of the outstanding couple remain in their many donations and in the Russell-Cotes Art Gallery and Museum with its comprehensive display of Victo-rian treasures in their former, elegant home. Lady Russell-Cotes' drawing room, her boudoir (where she died) and other rooms retain the charming atmosphere of Victorian prosperity and reflect the couple's love of acquiring unusual and splendid treasures, and above all, their great generosity and admiration for the town of Bournemouth.

BEATRICE WEBB

and THE FABIANS

The (P.C.) photo was taken by
George Bernard Shaw in 1908

Beatrice Potter, who became Beatrice Webb, and an important member of the Fabians, was born at Standish House, near Gloucester in 1858. Throughout her life she had many connections with the town of Bournemouth. She was the eighth daughter of a wealthy railway magnate with radical views. Beatrice was brought up in a liberal, political atmosphere whose father believed that women were more superior to men. She was educated informally by her father. At seventeen she was worried and undecided about many matters, religious and political. It was therefore decided to send her to a smart finishing school in Bournemouth, Standish House, which was situated in Bath Hill, (now a petrol station). and before she 'came out' into society at the age of eighteen. She found contact with the other girls difficult; they accepted ideas unquestioningly, while she had been brought up to think and reason for herself. She had always been encouraged to read widely and had travelled abroad with her parents, was intelligent, but could be moody and depressed at times.

At school she formed a strong friendship with her cousin, Margaret Harkness, both of whom felt uncertain on matters of Christianity. In Bournemouth, she attended the Holy Trinity Church (now an office block) where she was confirmed, and whose services she preferred to the High Church Tracterian views of St. Peter's Church. Some of the church doctrines continued to worry her, particularly atonement and the doctrine of sin.

On returning to the family home, suffering from headaches and other health problems, she made her entrance into society as a rather reluctant debutante and still with undecided views about religion. On meeting Joseph Chamberlain, a leading Liberal, she felt herself emotionally attracted to him.

A few years after the death of her mother in 1882, her father suffered a stroke. They decided to return to Bournemouth where they passed the next three winters in lodgings near the pier at a house which was near the Royal Bath Hotel, called Kildare (now a car park). Beatrice was happy there. She enjoyed pleasant cliff walks, the sea in all its moods, sea bathing which had just become popular and spectacular views of the Purbecks and the Isle of Wight. In between there were visits to London and visits from friends like T.H. Huxley and Herbert Spencer.

Although so wealthy, she was deeply concerned with conditions of poverty and poor housing. In her diary she wrote of socialism 'in which there will be individual freedom and public property instead of class slavery and private possession'. "At last I am a socialist," she wrote. When she wrote a letter on unemployment, it was later printed as an article in The Pall Mall Gazette which was read and approved by Joseph Chamberlain, to whom she felt attracted. He was a widower, a Liberal and an outstanding political figure, and like Beatrice supported better conditions for the working classes. He was also very ambitious and some of his beliefs upset Beatrice. He would expect to have complete authority over his wife and expect sympathetic understanding from her. Although she continued to enjoy his company she could not accept his views of domination. To Beatrice, his views demanded servility and that was completely unacceptable by her.

Whilst researching on the development of the co-operative movement, she met Sidney Webb, a Fabian theorist. At first she was far from impressed with the 28 years old man with a huge head covered in black hair and a large nose. In November 1890, he caught scarlet fever, and on Beatrice's recommendation, spent his convalescence in Bournemouth. He stayed at the Osborne Boarding House, opposite the Royal Exeter Hotel, walking and reading extensively while there. When he wrote of his affection for her, she replied that she would 'never make the stupendous sacrifice of marriage'.

She was appalled by conditions of poverty, researched into the East End Dock Life; she gave evidence to a House of Lord Committee on the 'Sweating System' after experiencing the terrible conditions herself by working for a time in a sweat shop.

In 1892 she married Sidney Webb, although she did not feel in love with him at first. Later she spoke of her enjoyment from her partner, lover and husband. In that year also the first Fabian Society was formed in Bournemouth with seven members and a secretary. The following year Beatrice became a Fabian herself.

In 1905 Beatrice was appointed to serve on the Royal Commission on the Poor Law. Conditions in workhouses were unpleasant; many people, even though starving, refused to go into the 'hated workhouse.' The Majority Report recommended more use of voluntary charity to relieve the destitute. But the Minority Report from Beatrice and Sidney Webb recommended the complete break up of the Poor Law and a more humane treatment of those in poor circumstances, also suggesting preventative measures. Beatrice's Minority Report resulted in the Beveridge Report of 1942 which was intended to cover people from birth to the grave, with health, education and care of destitute becoming essential, with an extension of all social services.

When Beatrice came to Bournemouth again to speak on her Minority Report at the old St. Peter's Hall, some objections were raised that the measures were too socialistic. Beatrice quickly retorted that if they intended by that then all public expenditure on prevention of destitution, poor law and health were socialistic. The Bournemouth Graphic wrote, "We can only hope that speedy success will crown Mrs. Webb's efforts."

In 1924 the Fabians, including Mr. and Mrs. Webb. were in Bournemouth staying at the Vegetarian Holiday Centre at St. Anthony's, Southbourne, and in 1926, the year of the General Strike, the TUC met in the Town Hall, Bournemouth.

There was another visit to Bournemouth in 1934 – for Beatrice – while Sidney went to Russia to complete his research for a book on the Soviet Union. It was the first time they had been separated for so long for 40 years. The letters she received from him were as loving and caring as in their early days of courtship. 'Kildare' the house where she had been so happy with her father was then still standing, and she still found pleasure from the sea and the golden sands, and the satisfaction from the publication of her first letter on unemployment. In 1937, both Webbs were back in Bournemouth to attend the Labour Party Conference at the Highcliff Hotel. The next Labour Conference at the Highcliff Hotel in 1940 was a distressing time with war, and the Germans invading Belgium and Holland.

As she grew older, her fame and works were more and more well known, and visitors came from afar to converse with the famous lady who had done so much for the country. When she was over 86, she again suffered from a kidney disease which had earlier in her life, been temporarily corrected. She died in 1943 and Sidney, who was awarded Order of Merit for 'eminent services to social and political science" died in 1947. Their ashes were originally buried in the garden of Passfield, near Hindhead in Surrey, their last home, but not for long. A letter in the Times from Bernard Shaw, a close friend and fellow Fabian, suggested that their ashes should be in Westminster Abbey. They were both great citizens whose work had enriched the country. It was the first time in 900 years that a man and his wife had been buried together at the same ceremony in Westminster Abbey. An address was given by Clement Atlee, another Fabian, who said, "Millions are living fuller and freer lives today because of the work of Sidney and Beatrice Webb."

Their intelligence, caring, kindness, a happy marriage for over 40 years, their work for the Welfare State, their founding of the London School of Economics, the list is endless. The memories of these two great people will be honoured for many years to come.

FLORENCE VAN RAALTE

– FROM EDWARDIAN SPLENDOUR TO COMPLETE SOLITUDE

Although visited by thousands of visitors each year, Brownsea is still a secret island with an atmosphere of its own, not found in the mainland, a miniature world inside the mainland. At one time it was part of the Manor of Studland, and since the 16th century up to the last world war has played an important part in the defence of the south coast.

The island has had many owners, some eccentric, some amazingly wealthy, while two became bankrupt. But it is the ladies this article is concerned with. In 1901 an era of elegant splendour commenced with the purchase of the island by Charles Van Raalte and his wife Florence, a wealthy, charming and talented couple. Entertainments were plentiful and lavish and many members of royalty joined their magnificent banquets and house parties, including the Queen of Roumania with her family who spent a summer on the island. Marconi was a frequent visitor to the island, mooring his famous yacht, 'Elettra' by the island and taking part in the fun and gaiety of the island. There was golfing and shooting while the island became more and more self-supporting, providing the needs of the castle on the island. In the glasshouses and kitchen gardens there were luscious peaches, nectarines and grapes and a wide variety of other fruits and vegetables. There was a staff of about 30 and 10 gardeners looked after the grounds of the castle. (The castle was built in the 16th century, later destroyed by fire and rebuilt in 1901).

Mrs. Van Raalte was an accomplished artist in water colour and had often exhibited her paintings in galleries in London. She was responsible for many of the improvements to the castle, excelling in tasteful furnishings and the display of fine pictures. Twenty musicians played every evening on the castle lawns or in the great hall to entertain the distinguished couple and their many guests. In 1907 Florence permitted Robert Baden Powell to hold a camp there for about 20 boys, when the boy scout movement was born at Brownsea.

Sadly, Charles Van Raalte died in January 1908. For 15 years after his death the elegant Florence kept the estate in good condition and continued to entertain her wealthy friends and nobility, but in 1925 she left the island.

The Castle, Brownsea Island

MRS. MARY FLORENCE BONHAM CHRISTIE

The days of splendour were over when the island was purchased by the last private owner in 1927, Mrs. Mary Florence Bonham Christie, another wealthy lady, but vastly different from Mrs. Van Raalte. A new steward was appointed and the islanders were made to leave. There was much sadness as many of the families of islanders had lived at Brownsea for generations. The population was reduced from 270 to 4! Farming and commercial enterprises ceased; bats occupied the church and the pews became covered with thick dust. Under her 'reign' the island became a truly secret and forbidden island when practically all relations with the outside world were terminated. Strangely, she allowed 500 scouts to visit the island to celebrate the jubilee of their movement, but the plant life was slowly taking over the island which was becoming wilder and more overgrown. There was trouble for anyone who tried to land on the island. When a tailor and his daughter landed on the island to dig for bait, they were surprised to be confronted by Mrs. Christie who angrily informed them that if they returned her servants would have orders to throw them and their belongings into the sea.

Perhaps stubbornly, they returned, in 1933, when a huge, Amazonian blond appeared in front of them and ordered them off the island. There was an angry tussle with a boatman who also appeared, while the Teutonic Amazonian female seized the daughter and threw her into the water. The tailor, more angry again, brought a case against this huge blond woman who was fined 40/-. She announced to the court that she was Scandinavian, a fully qualified physical training instructor and was hired to keep all intruders off the island and to work on the land.

After that no one dared to land on the island, even Peter Scott was refused permission to make a film of the amazing bird and plant life on the island. Nature was allowed to repossess the island, wondrous coloured peacocks strolled majestically and contentedly through the overgrown paths, displaying their magnificent feathers in fan-like shapes; flowers and rhododendrons thrived and multiplied; there were numerous birds, red squirrels and many other animals, but there were also mosquitoes and oversized rats! Everything else was allowed to decay, including the village, the church and the public house. A caretaker and game-keeper lived on the island, The only other visitors permitted were members of her own family, a couple who cleaned the castle and the postman. Mrs. Christie lived in one of the castle rooms, not even bothering to unpack many of her belongings. She did her own cooking on oil stoves.

But the peace of the island was shattered by the second World War when Royal Navy and other service personnel, Dutch and Belgian refugees, many distraught and afraid, were billeted on the island. Some of the soldiers were uncouth and even killed some of the peacocks and ate them, while the birds became fearful for the first time in their lives and hid in dense parts of the island. Mrs. Christie who loved all birds and beasts was horrified when she realised what was happening and, in distress, she wept.

After the war the island reverted to its secrecy and became again an island of peace and tranquillity where nature thrived, plants and trees spread in a thick maze of overgrown bushes and sprawling, intertwining branches. In 1961, Mrs. Christie then 98 years old, became ill and had to leave her beloved island. She died in April that year in a Nursing Home in Branksome Park. There were then only two other people living on the island. Her ashes were scattered on Brownsea among the plants and birds she had cared for. Brownsea was left to her grandson who presented it to the Treasury to pay for death duties. The Treasury, in turn, presented the island to the National Trust who own it today. £100,000 was needed to repair buildings and restore the wilderness and overgrown woods into a pleasant island which could again be open to the public.

The beauty of Brownsea, the semi-tame, brilliantly coloured peacocks who strut placidly around the island, red squirrels, a variety of other animals and birds give pleasure to many people today, while tales of Mrs. Christie abound and prove her to be a completely individualistic person who loved animals, birds and trees and who did not care much for the human specie.

GEORGINA AND MARIANNE TALBOT
OF TALBOT VILLAGE

Georgina Talbot

Talbot Village is unique – a well-wooded, secluded sanctuary which adjoins the busy, noisy, Wallisdown Road. This delightful village owes its existence to two wonderful, philanthropic ladies of the Victorian era, the Misses Georgina and Marianne Talbot. When they moved from London to Bournemouth in 1842, Georgina, the elder of the two, was horrified by the abject poverty of those times. Tired, worn out families used to crowd outside the windows of their House on the East Cliff calling out, "We are starving, we want work."

Georgina, greatly moved and deeply concerned, decided, at no cost to the town, to help to improve conditions. She purchased 465 acres of land from Sir George Gervis, the Lord of the Manor, which she turned into a self-supporting village for unemployed workers who were prepared to maintain themselves and their families by their own efforts.

There were certain rules. No trades were allowed, except for the sale of poultry, eggs and bacon, Six farms were constructed (most of which have disappeared in urban development). There were 16 well constructed cottages, all detached, and having one acre of land. Each house had a well and a pig sty, and rents were low, about four shillings per week. The village was non-denominational, based on the precepts, 'Love God, Keep the Commandments and Honour the Queen'. In 1862 seven attractive almshouses were constructed for those old and unable to work. They had their own flower gardens, a vegetable patch, pigsty and a space for poultry. And above all they had peace and security with no fear of the dreaded workhouse.

In 1862 also a village school was constructed, which opened with 68 children in attendance who were to be instructed in reading, writing, arithmetic and scripture. A deed of settlement of 1883 granted the sum of £66 'so long as the portrait of Georgina Talbot shall be hung in the schoolroom'. The provisions of the school were changed with the passing of the 1944 Education Act, but the beautiful portrait still has its place of honour in the school, which today has been considerably extended and modernized. By 1870 there was a new church, St. Marks Church, built of Portland and Purbeck stone. Unfortunately the kind Georgina died before the consecration of the church and was the first to be buried in the spacious churchyard. An inscription round the fine Ionic Memorial Cross reads:

'She came of an ancient race, and possessed in herself that nobility of mind which delighted in the happiness of her fellow creatures ... In the neighbourhood of this village she passed 25 years of a blameless life, giving up time and fortune to bettering the conditions of the poorer classes, seeking to minister to their temporal and spiritual welfare and erecting habitations suitable to their positions in life, herself enjoying a peaceful and happy existence in doing good.'

After the death of Georgina, her sister Marianne arranged for the completion of the church, adding a gracefully proportioned pulpit and an ancient font and other gifts. For many years Marianne continued the policy adopted by her sister, which also permitted access to the beautiful Talbot woods. Even today anyone can stroll along the paths in the Village and enjoy the magnificent woodland scenery. When Marianne died in 1885, another memorial cross was erected, the inscription extolling her kind and affectionate nature and her love of beauty and goodness which endeared her to her many friends through her long and excellent life.

The work of these two ladies is still revered and respected whilst Talbot Village remains as a sanctuary of beauty and peacefulness off a busy main road and growing industrial area.

ALMA RATHENBURY

A CRIME OF PASSION

The residents of select, tree-lined Manor Road. Bournemouth were horrified when they learned that their neighbour, Mrs. Rattenbury, a brilliant musician and composer, had been accused of the murder of her husband, Francis, a distinguished, retired architect. It seemed incredible that his charming wife, Alma, could actually have smashed her husband's head with a mallet, causing injuries so severe that he died shortly afterwards. But this was only the beginning of the amazing story which hit the headlines in 1935, when shocking tales of scandalous behaviour were made public.

Traumatic, talented and tragic, sums up much of the life of Alma Rattenbury, accomplished pianist, violinist, singer and composer.

Her father, a German immigrant, named Wolfe, a gold mining prospector, lived roughly in the Canadian Rockies and Alaska, but when a daughter was born about 1898 his English wife left the hard life and settled in Victoria, the capital of British Columbia. After her husband disappeared after one of his mining excursions she remarried and the young girl became known as Alma Clarke, when she was described by one of her teachers as an outstandingly clever child . . . full of music and happiness. From Junior School she was sent to an exclusive girls' school in Toronto. Her ambitious mother insisted that she practised music for several hours each day. From eight years old the young girl performed in concerts and gave recitals and was soon known as 'an infant prodigy' for her music on both the piano and violin. Delighted audiences enjoyed her rendering of classical music while the Toronto Globe commented on her exceptional talent and the brilliancy of her musical ability. By the time she was 17 she had appeared with the Toronto Symphony Orchestra as both a piano and violin soloist, and had begun composing romantic songs, usually written on the back of envelopes.

Her attractive appearance and pleasant manners brought her many boy friends. But by 1913 her first real love entered her life in the form of a handsome Irishman, Caledon Dolling who came from an important Catholic family and whose grandfather was High Sheriff of Londonderry. As Alma was not a Catholic, her mother strongly opposed the marriage resulting in an elopement and marriage in 1914. Radiantly happy, their marital bliss was marred by the outbreak of the First World War, when Caledon and his brother both enlisted. To be near her husband, Alma accompanied him and performed in numerous concerts for the troops, and when he was posted to England, she obtained a post at the War Office in London. Unfortunately he was next sent to France when he was twice wounded, and in August 1916 he was killed. Heartbroken, Alma left London and commenced work with a branch of the French Red Cross at Royaumont, sometimes working behind the lines as an orderly and stretcher bearer, also in the hope of finding her husband's grave. For her bravery – Alma was twice wounded – she was awarded Croix de Guerre with star and palm.

The loss of her husband, her first great love, left her feeling bitter and cynical. When she met Captain Compton Pakenham who had been awarded the Military Cross for his bravery, and who was a man of charm, distantly related to the Earl of Longford, they became friends. Captain Pakenham was already married. It was said that Alma lived with him resulting in her being cited in their divorce case in 1920. In 1921 they married and soon had a son named Christopher. For a time they lived in Long Island, America where Pakenham worked as a book reviewer and lectured on economy. Alma gave piano lessons to help to overcome their lack of money, but their financial condition worsened and the marriage failed. Alma who had quarrelled with her mother over her first marriage, in desperation wrote to her asking for help. Her mother responded to her plea and came speedily to America and took Alma and Christopher back with her to British Columbia.

It was the first time that Alma had returned to her native city since her marriage to Dolling. After staying with her mother for a period she rented a small house when she taught the piano and gave recitals in an endeavour to earn money for herself and her son. Good looking, lively, talented, she soon became well known in the social circles in Victoria.

After one of her recitals at the Empress Hotel, she heard cheering and singing in the adjoining dining room, and was told it was to honour a famous architect, Francis Mawson Rattenbury, who had designed that particular hotel. He was tall, handsome, and about 30 years older than Alma. Although so popular she still had a feeling of loneliness and felt attracted to the clever, tall architect. He was married, but the marriage was not successful. The attraction was mutual for the two disillusioned people. During a dance to which he had invited Alma, she looked at this tall escort and murmured, to his surprise, that he had a lovely face and that it was the kindest face she had ever seen.

Rattenbury had trained as an architect in his native Yorkshire. In 1892 he left England for British Columbia where he entered a competition to prove a design for a new Parliament building. To his great surprise and pleasure he was declared the winner. From that time his career as a prominent architect flourished. Other buildings were designed by him and wealthy people often requested his services. He also designed a new, portable house.

In 1898 the opening of the new parliament was celebrated. It was greatly admired by most people and criticized by some because of its high cost. As the work had dominated his life, he had spent less time at home, with the result that Florrie, his wife and Francis drifted further and further apart. Suddenly he lost interest in his achievements and became tired and morose. It was at this stage that he met Alma whose magnetic personality soon revived the ageing architect. With difficulty, and even unkind treatment, he persuaded Florrie to divorce him, and for the second time Alma was named as co-respondent. Bewitched and happy he married his lovely lady and brought Alma and her son to his palatial home in Oak Bay. Alma was thrilled to be living in such a lovely home, but soon began to feel ill, and after unsuccessful treatment from various doctors, an abscess on the brain was discovered and treated by a chiropractor who had formerly successfully treated Frances.

In 1925, about two months after their marriage and in a letter to his sister he wrote of his happiness, and described Emma as looking like a fragile Madonna, but full of fun – a bright and loveable companion. He added "I can't imagine life without her now." Family quarrels arose with Rattenbury's relatives showing their disapproval of his new marriage and sympathizing with poor Florrie, followed by disputes with the Canadian Government over land which he had purchased in 1907. An acrimonious court case followed which resulted in his defeat and the loss of much of his fortune.

When their son John was born Alma wanted him to be baptised at the family church in Okehampton. Life had become unpleasant and although Rattenbury had donated land in British Columbia for public use he was still neglected and unpopular. With some sadness he left Canada for a new life in England. Before settling in England they spent an interesting year travelling from one country to another. In Venice Alma was thrilled to visit Gigli's palazzo. Her attractive appearance soon attracted scores of Italian males who followed her with their chorus of 'Bella, bella.' Arriving in England they went to Okehampton where little John was baptized. They decided to make their home in Bournemouth, similar in many ways to Victoria, with its Victorian atmosphere and stylish villas and where Alma would have the great pleasure of hearing the famous Bourne-mouth Symphony Orchestra. They rented the Villa Madeira near the cliffs and with a good sea view, and when Alma's grand piano arrived, her joy was complete.

Songs and melodies were jotted down on scraps of paper, while Ratz (as Alma called him) endeavoured, without success, to find a publisher until he contacted Sir Dan Godfrey who was responsible for the Bournemouth Symphony Orchestra and who advised them to contact Keith Prowse in London. The head of the firm, after hearing some of Alma's songs, was most impressed and agreed to publish one number and have it orchestrated and broadcast and keep two others for the piano. They were both thrilled and Ratz was particularly pleased that Alma was again on the road to fame. Mr. Van Lier, the head, praised Alma as a marvellous

65

person with a mind full of exquisite tunes. Two hundred compositions a week were submitted to the publishers, many of which were rejected, but there he was praising Alma as a genius and prepared to spend large sums of money on promoting her work. At the Mayfair Hotel they met the band leader, Ambrose, who would broadcast some of her music.

Alma took the name Lozanne and soon had written a series of songs, 'Zanita'.

Later she met the tenor, Frank Titterton, and he, too, was delighted to sing her songs. Life was good. Alma and Ratz were happy. She loved her children dearly. Often they went into the New Forest where she would play her violin to them or they would play merrily on the beach and splash in the sea. John was attending a day school and then became a weekly boarder. Alma's life was full. She wore smart, fashionable clothes; they had a Daimler and paid frequent visits to London, but sometimes neighbours regarded her with suspicion because of her erratic life style and late hours as she sometimes played and composed music until the early hours of the morning.

At this stage Ratz seemed to lose interest in both Alma and her music. He was concerned with a new scheme for the construction of a block of flats, but the scheme caused him much worry and he became more and more depressed. Alma, always very affable, found a new friend in Irene Riggs who she employed as companion/housekeeper. Alma who was never class-conscious and always kind, soon regarded Irene as an equal. Together they enjoyed shopping trips and other excursions.

In 1932 Alma fell ill and TB was diagnosed, but this did not prevent her from beginning to drink cocktails. Her husband's indifference began to affect her adversely while he became more worried about their financial condition. Her generosity which used to please him began to annoy him especially as she was careless with money. Although she received a generous allowance of £1,000 a year, this had to cover household expenses, clothes, staff and school fees, as well as the doctor's fees, who as a friend and doctor was often in attendance. Sometimes she was overdrawn from the Bank and to obtain more money from Ratz she began to invent imaginary problems. Money from Record Companies was quickly spent even though her successes were increasing all the time, and in 1935 there was a special performance of her music on the radio. Rattenbury continued to feel despondent and gloomy and even threatened to commit suicide. Alma, irritated, said 'Why don't you?' A row ensued and, deeply annoyed, he struck her face. She retaliated and bit his arm, when he dashed out of the house. Upset, Alma called Dr. O'Donnell who bathed her black eye, gave her a small dose of morphia. With police assistance they looked for Rattenbury on the cliffs, but about 2 a.m., he returned.

Alma, again, had more health problems and underwent several operations for TB glands. As Francis no longer wished to drive the car, they advertised for a young boy who would help in the house, the garden and drive the car, when they engaged George Percy Stoner, a pleasant, good looking youth, who claimed to be 22 year old – of limited education and from a working class background. Alma quickly accepted him as an equal and as a member of the of the family. Soon he was smoking Rattenbury's cigars, playing cards with him and even discussed his business problems, He was paid £1 per week and became the regular chauffeur/gardener in the house.

As Rattenbury became more hermit-like and gloomy, Alma relied more and more on the young Stoner for drives with Irene to the country, shopping and even to London. Alma who had been starved of passion, emotion and sexual attachment since the birth of little John, felt attracted to the young boy who reminded her of her first great love, who was so tragically killed in the war, while the young man, simple in many ways, unsophisticated, was overwhelmed by the kindness and affection of his attractive mistress. Irene, unhappy about possible unfortunate events, realised that the pair had become lovers, and especially after Alma arranged for him to 'live in' in the Villa. Who made the first advances? It must have been the older woman, three times married who besides being his mistress, had become his mistress in both senses of the word.

As a result of Stoner's sexual acceptance by his mistress, Stoner became domineering and self-assertive. But when Alma discovered that he was only 18 she half-heartedly tried to break off their relationship. A furious quarrel broke out and Stoner, jealous, lost his temper and tightened his grip round Alma, when Irene who had heard them, had to intervene. Another time he threatened to strangle her, which he explained by saying that he was taking drugs, and on another occasion he told her he felt impelled to throw himself from a train as it crossed the River Avon near Christchurch. This strange remark stayed in Alma's mind for a long time.

To persuade Rattenbury to give her more money, as she was considerably overdrawn at the Bank, she told him she must go to London for an operation. As she had had previous ones it seemed a reasonable request. Reluctantly Ratz gave her £250 with which she paid some outstanding debts and made swift arrangements to travel to London with Stoner for a few days.

On arrival in London, Alma signed the register at the Royal Palace Hotel as Mrs. Rattenbury and brother. Although she booked two single rooms, their sexual delights continued. During the day a great spending spree took place as Alma purchased for her lover 3 pairs of crepe-de-chine pyjamas, silk shirts and other items. Stoner, with some of her money, purchased a ring for his lady-love. They spent three memorable days shopping, theatre-going and wandering round London.

On returning to Bournemouth, Ratz was already in bed and merry with whisky and asked no questions about the supposed operation.

The following morning, Rattenbury was again suffering from depression and insisted on reading aloud a threatened suicide passage from the book he was reading, and afterwards remarked that it was better to kill yourself than become feeble minded. To distract him, Alma suggested a visit to a business friend at Bridport and with whom he could discuss the problems concerning the block of flats in which he was interested.

On 23rd March, Francis was still depressed, but played his usual game of cards with Alma, who later told Irene of the proposed visit to Bridport. Later that night Irene heard the distraught voice of Alma, screaming for her. She rushed downstairs and saw to her horror Rattenbury lolling in his chair, blood pouring from his hair and face and pools of blood on the carpet. He was quite unconscious, while Alma frantically rubbed his hands. She cried to Irene to get a doctor as someone had hurt Ratz. Alma, as if she did not know what she was doing, wrapped a towel around Rattenbury's head, seized a whisky bottle and poured herself a drink and then a second. Irene bathed his eye which had become black. They tried to lift him but he was much too heavy to lift and they called for Stoner to help them. Between them they managed to get the unconscious man on to his bed. All this time Alma was talking in an incoherent manner, then she worried about little John, asleep in her bedroom. He must not see the blood. Frantically she tried to clean it up.

When Dr. O'Donnell arrived, he realised the seriousness of the wounds and telephoned for Mr. Rooke, a surgeon, who lived nearby. Alma, quite distraught, tried to remove some of her husband's clothes, talking all the time and getting in the way of the surgeon. Quickly he phoned for an ambulance and made arrangements for him to be taken to the Strathallen Nursing Home, when three wounds were discovered on the left side of his head, which could only have been caused by a violent attack. O'Donnell phoned the police.

Alma continued to drink, and when the policeman arrived, she was still talking nonsensically and still playing loud music and seemed in a drunken haze. Suddenly she announced, "I know who did it. I did it with a mallet". She added that the mallet was hidden. Then the story was changed and she explained that it was her lover who had done it, then changing again, added that it was Rattenbury's son who had done it, although he was living in Canada. Staggering all over the place, talking more and more nonsense, Dr. O'Donnell decided to take her to her bedroom and gave her half a grain of morphia, a few minutes later she had come down again, and for a second time the doctor took her back, telling the police that she was not in a fit condition to be questioned. This time she slept. Police-detectives arrived and a police matron. When Alma awoke she felt sick and couldn't hold the cup of coffee which was given to her, without help. Suddenly the mallet was found with blood and hairs sticking to it, and Alma was charged with 'attempted murder.' Before they took her away she whispered to Irene, "Tell Stoner he must give me the mallet," forgetting that it was already in police hands.

When she left in the police car she became even more upset as she became aware of her little boy, pale with anxiety, staring uncomprehendingly at her.

At Bournemouth Police Station she was warned and charged with 'Attempted Murder', when she replied, "That's right. I did it deliberately and I'd do it again." At the Magistrates Court, and on the advice of her solicitor, she pleaded 'Not Guilty'. When the doctor was allowed to see her, he was further shocked. She could hardly stand, was swaying all the time, her eyes were screwed up and she was very worried about what would happen to her children. Shortly afterwards she was sent to the Royal Holloway Prison for women. Headlines appeared in the Daily Echo EAST CLIFF SENSATION, WOMAN IN THE DOCK, ATTEMPTED MURDER CHARGE, REMANDED FOR EIGHT DAYS. The paper also noted that the woman seemed dazed and was allowed to sit down during the short hearing.

At Holloway her mind was still in a whirl; she kept thinking of the awful moment when she discovered Francis, when she had stumbled on his false teeth and on feeling sick. It was like an awful nightmare. The first time she saw the governor, she was still under the influence of morphia. The second time, he found that she had hardly any recollection of the immediate past, but kept reiterating sadly, "It was my fault."

After Irene had taken the little boy back to school, she, together with Stoner, decided to get away from the house for a while and go to Wimborne. On the return journey, he admitted that he killed his employer, that he was jealous, had seen Rattenbury making love to Alma, and was worried that they would share the same room together at Bridport. That evening he became drunk, shouting "Mrs. Rattenbury is in jail and I put her there." He would go to London the next day to see Alma and then would give himself up. When Dr. O'Donnell called at the house, with some hesitation, Irene told him of the new development. The police were informed and Stoner was arrested at Bournemouth Station on his return, disappointed not to have been able to see Alma.

He was shocked and shaken when he was informed that his employer had died while he was in London, and the charge had become one of murder. As there were now two confessions of guilt, both were charged with the murder, followed by a hearing in Bournemouth, when a queue, consisting mostly of women, shocked, horrified and inquisitive, gathered outside the law courts in Stafford Road. The case was remanded and they were both committed for trial at the Central Criminal Court in London.

For a time, Alma persisted in her assertion that she was responsible for her husband's death, in order to protect the young man she loved passionately. It was only after strong persuasion from a close relative that she realised the problems and unhappiness that would be caused to her two children if she were imprisoned for a long time, or even hanged. Reluctantly she admitted that the crime was committed by Stoner and not by herself, and that he was jealous of their proposed visit to Bridport and where he thought they would be sharing the same bedroom.

Vivid and startling headlines spread the news throughout England. During the long, exhaustive trial with the crowds both inside and outside the Old Bailey getting larger all the time, it was seen that Mrs. Rattenbury aged perceptibly and that her main anxiety concerned the fate of George Stoner. It was also noticeable that the sympathy of the crowd was with the young, eighteen years old youth who had been seduced by his much older mistress.

When Stoner was declared guilty and the death sentence pronounced, Alma, ashen white, staggered and almost fainted, tears ran down her face, as she held on to two wardresses who prevented her from falling. Although exonerated herself, she had been severely criticised by the judge for her disgusting immorality and adulterous behaviour, particularly with a servant and such a young one.

Unhappy, desperate and worn out by probing, antagonistic questions, Alma was taken by friends to a nursing home. En route she was continually harassed and followed by reporters and photographers eager for any newsworthy remarks that might slip from her lips.

In the nursing home she was heard to murmur that when her lover was hanged she would kill herself. Sadly she hummed the words of one of her little compositions:

> We have lived together,
> We two; We have loved together,
> I and you. We'll die together,
> You and I – We'll swing together.

Almost besides herself with grief, bewildered and anxious to get away from the hostile crowds, she suddenly left the nursing home, without telling anyone and caught a train for Bournemouth. Distraught, grief-stricken, she strolled by the River Avon, walking through the meadows, golden with spring flowers. By the railway bridge and Three Arches, she stopped and sat down. On the back of an old envelope she scribbled some rough notes, asking her friends to care for her children, explaining sadly that there was no life left for her as her lover was to die, and that her name had been blackened for all times, by the Judge's and the press pitiless condemnation of her. Taking a knife she had previously purchased, she waded into the water, like distressed Ophelia, and stabbed herself six times. When her body was recovered she was taken to the Public Assistance Institute at Fairmile House, Christchurch.

Headlines in the papers read: MRS. RATTENBURY STABBED AND DROWNED, ACQUITTED BUT SELF-CONDEMNED. The Evening News commented that she was nearly 43 and that she had obviously been crushed by the Judge's severe remarks. The Bournemouth Times commenced: 'The last tragic moments of the life of Mrs. Alma Rattenbury have done something to mitigate, if not condone her guilt in a human drama, the terrible consequences of which could never have been foreseen.'

The funeral took place at Cemetery Junction in Bournemouth, and although attempts had been made to keep it secret, one thousand people, mostly women, attended, some to sympathize and others to vilify, while her home in Manor Road was raided by avaricious souvenir hunters.

As for Stoner, his sentence, on appeal, was commuted to life imprisonment, despite 320,000 signatures appealing for clemency on grounds of his youth and the unfortunate influence of an older woman. As a model prisoner, he was released after seven years, in 1942. He immediately joined the Forces. After the war, he settled down, later married and continued to live in the south of England.

About 1940, the Villa Madeira was purchased by an Austrian couple who had fled from Nazi oppression. Their first knowledge of the murder was when a visiting electrician remarked casually, "I hope they mopped all the blood."

It is said that on cold, windy nights a slim figure glides through the garden, said to be Alma, looking for her two children and at the home which brought her both days of pleasure and great unhappiness.

The house in Manor Road

EDITH AND ELLEN COOPER DEAN

and the end of a GREAT FAMILY

Ellen Cooper Dean

The Dean family were originally yeoman farmers who lived in Holdenhurst from about 1690. Over the years they built up a fortune; with others they founded the Christchurch, Wimborne and Ringwood Bank, and owned considerable amounts of land in Holdenhurst and throughout Bournemouth and for many years have been generous benefactors to the town they helped to develop. By marriage, the name 'Cooper' was attached to 'Dean.'. How very sad that by 1984 this ancient line had become extinct after the deaths of the last two remaining members, the unmarried daughters, Ellen and Edith Cooper Dean.

Littledown House, a solid, massive Georgian house was built in the late 18th century by William Dean on an elevated area of rough, overgrown heathland on the Great Dean Common near Holdenhurst. A smaller house on the site had been previously owned by his father, John Dean.

On the death of James Cooper Dean in 1921, his wealth and the house passed to his son, Joseph, sometimes known as 'The Squire of Bournemouth', and the father of Ellen and Edith Cooper Dean.

The two girls were sent, but for a short time only, to two private schools – Ellen to Grovely Manor, Boscombe, and Edith to a private school in Lychett Matravers. When their mother became ill, Ellen, the elder, shy and diffident, stayed at home to care for her. The two girls were different in character. Edith was tall, domineering and good-looking. It has been said that these girls, members of an extremely wealthy family should have had a full and active life among the society of those days, while, instead, their lives were quiet and restricted to the country around them. On the death of their mother, they cared for their father, with Ellen being responsible for the domestic arrangements at Littledown, while Edith helped her father with the Littledown and Holdenhurst farms.

It was thought that Edith, the younger of the two girls, would probably meet a farmer or landowner at the markets or agricultural shows that she attended, and that she would then have sons to carry on the family line. It was a great shock to all, when after a period of ill-health she was informed that she would never be able to have children. Sadly she turned her back on marriage. If she could not have children she would not think again of marriage. She developed a harder side to her nature and even felt jealous of her sister to whom the hopes of the family now turned. But Ellen, quiet, unassuming, had her own opinions, and decided that she would only marry if someone she really cared for came along.

Her father's attitude was strange. Although he wanted her to marry, he would suspect young men of being after their money and used to treat them coldly. A friendship with a young bank clerk was immediately discouraged. He actually said to Ellen, "You can't marry him and that's an end to that." Later there was a friendship with a young RAF Officer who was stationed near Bournemouth. They found they had many interests in common and often met for dinner and dances, and Joseph actually approved of him. Unfortunately he was killed in a flying accident. Poor Ellen, she was distraught and slowly, like her sister, turned her back on marriage.

Looking after the house was still left in the charge of Ellen, while Edith continued to run the estate with her father. There had been tension between the two sisters for some time, and Ellen, then 33, had looked after the big house for over 10 years. She then realised that she must get away and have a life of her own. Luckily she had a friend, Jay Wilson, to whom she suggested that they bought a house and lived there together. It seems strange that belonging to such a wealthy family, the sisters should have little money of their own. Reluctantly she turned to her father who agreed to lend her the money on an interest free mortgage. A house was purchased at Milford-on-Sea in, what they considered, an ideal position near the sea. At first it was delightful, but winter came and angry, tempestuous seas suddenly flooded their house. Quickly they got away and quickly they sold the house and bought another in New Milton, naming it Little Dene in memory of her old home.

Meanwhile, Edith invited an old friend and former nurse, Cecily Appleby, known as 'Apple' to stay with her, look after the domestic arrangements and care for her elderly father, while she managed the farms. In 1938, Joseph Cooper Dean was 72 and he began to realise that the end of the family was approaching. To ensure that the sisters were well provided for, he made over to them some of his major estates on the West Cliff, the remainder of Northwood and Eastwood estates and Manor Farm in Holdenhurst. For the first time in their lives the sisters had property and an income of their own.

When the Second World War broke out, the girls took an active part, Edith as a VAD nurse while Ellen and Jay joined the WVS. Ellen bought and equipped a mobile canteen, and often worked in soldiers' units in the New Forest. Ellen enjoyed her work, and her friendly manner and reliability were greatly appreciated.

Shortly after the war, the two friends, both suffering from ill-health, moved into the Carlton Hotel, Bournemouth, where Ellen's two elderly aunts were also living. Joseph died in 1950 and the rest of the Dean estates and investments came to the sisters. Edith continued to live at Littledown and enjoyed pleasant holidays abroad. But Ellen and Jay, at the Carlton, felt lonely and outcast, especially when Jay became a permanent invalid. Ellen, whose health had suffered during the war, spent most of her time looking after her friend, who died in 1966. Ellen was even more lonely in the past.

Ellen had, for many years, been interested in horse racing. Through treatment for arthritis by a clever physiotherapist, Miss Sylvia Bowditch, a friendship developed and the new friend was also interested in racing. A holiday in Ireland together improved Ellen's health problems. To Ellen, it was like a new world opening, with the excitement of visits to races, stables and studs. There was a visit to Ascot and successful bets, and the great joy of holidays abroad. A thought which had lain dormant for some time, came to the fore again. She would like to own her own race horse and a farm of her own.

With her new friend, Ellen had been able to spend and had bought favourite paintings and fashionable clothes, and again there was a money problem. It was suggested that they sell Littledown House and its 163 acres of parkland to Bournemouth Corporation. (Ellen was then 73 and Edith was 70). A price of £2,640,000 was agreed to be paid over a period of eight years, interest free, beginning in 1973. The sisters would be able to live in the House until 31st March 1984 and if they remained after that time they would pay interest at 7%. With some sadness the sisters signed relinquishment of the family home since 1798. Edith and Apple intended to carry on farming until the last fixed date.

Ellen was able to buy Parnham Park Farm with 730 acres and in 1974 bought her first horse. The benevolence of the Cooper Deans is well known, and Ellen and Edith continued this generosity, Edith forming the Edith Cooper Dean Foundation and preventing the closure of the Uplands School, Poole, by purchasing the site of the school and paying for new buildings. When Ellen heard that the Hants County Cricket Club needed a new Score Board at the Dean Park Cricket ground, she gladly paid for a new one, and when she heard that the Stable Lads Welfare Trust had financial problems, she immediately made a gift of money to the Trust. The racing continued and she purchased more horses, but advanced arthritis made journeys difficult.

Edith was happy farming and seemed in good health, so it was a shock to her friends when she died suddenly after a heart attack. Ellen was then the only member left of the Cooper Dean family. She went back to Littledown House, happy to manage it again, until the departure date in 1984, and, not wishing to lose Parnham, she travelled weekly between the two houses. To help those less well off or sick and for the advancement of education and religion and other charitable purposes, she founded the Alice Ellen Cooper Dean Foundation. With three farms to manage, her life was full and with the help of Sylvia they entered and won several competitions, also raising and managing pedigree cattle.

A heart attack in 1982 caused her to live quietly at Parnham and leave Littledown. Ellen died on 14th April 1984 and was buried with other members of her family at Holdenhurst. As George Bruce states in his detailed book on the Life and Fortunes of the Family, 'Holdenhurst, from whence they originated, is called The Forgotten Village. Let them not become the FORGOTTEN FAMILY' Their generosity to Bournemouth and area, past, present and future, through the family Trusts should ensure that the name COOPER DEAN will never be forgotten.

MRS. YORKE BATLEY, AN AMAZING LADY

(not forgetting her husband)

A television programme on BBC South aroused my interest in an amazing lady who lived in Boscombe, Bournemouth for over 40 years, and entertained over 10,000 members of the theatrical profession to tea parties at her house.

Who could this person be, and how did she become an established favourite with the many entertainers and actors who appeared in Bournemouth? During a pleasant interview, Mrs. Yorke Batley, a charming white-haired lady explained the mystery and gave me details of some of the interesting events in the life of herself and her husband.

During the first World War, Mr. Batley became chaplain to the troops. For his work of rescuing and helping wounded soldiers, he was awarded the Military Cross.

After the war, and in his parish at Crockham Hill, he also taught part time, which he enjoyed very much. As a result he bought a preparatory school in 1924, the Wychwood School in Bournemouth, in partnership with J.B. Calkin, an eminent Archaeologist who has made many wonderful discoveries in that famous mound of antiquity, Hengistbury Head. Many well-known people attended the school, including several members of the well known Beale family of Bournemouth, Group Captain Peter Townsend, who hoped to marry Princess Margaret, and also Gerald Durrell, animal lover and writer, who hoped to open a zoo in Bournemouth. In 1938 the school was sold and in the early seventies the building with its turrets and towers, was acquired for demolition and redevelopment.

When Mr. Yorke Batley left the school, he was asked to return to parish work and offered a living in Corfe Castle. In 1948 he retired and came back to Bournemouth, buying a house in Boscombe, 'Kits Close' which became well known as the house where theatricals were entertained. How did this come about?

After they had been in the area for a short time, they received a visit from the Rural Dean who asked Mr. Batley if he would become the Actors' Church Union Chaplain at the Pavilion Theatre, Bournemouth. As he had never had any connections with the theatre, he was more than astonished by the request and was hesitant about accepting. But the Rural Dean assured him that there would be no problems. He had merely to go to the Pavilion and discuss any difficulties or worries experienced by the performers. The Church Union was aiming to appoint a chaplain in all major towns to give advice and assistance to artistes.

To make friendly contact with the artistes appearing in the town, they decided to give tea parties in their home. Being retired they had more time than the Vicar of a busy parish.

A routine was worked out. On Mondays they went to the theatre to meet the Company Manager and find how many artistes were performing that week. Monday evening they saw the show and afterwards went back stage to meet the actors who were then invited to a tea party on the following Friday afternoon. These occasions were often lively and jolly and many friendships were formed. The artistes who spend most of their time travelling from one place to another appreciated the welcoming atmosphere and the home comforts.

Sadly, Mr. Yorke Batley died in 1960 and his wife felt that she could not continue on her own and without his support. Shortly afterwards, Leslie Crowther, one of their earliest friends, came to see her. He persuaded her to continue to entertain the artistes who came to the Pavilion. Her friendship and the invitations to her home in Boscombe were greatly appreciated. Hotel rooms and flats were impersonal and often lonely and the artistes had little opportunity for social contact away from rehearsals and performances.

With some trepidation, and feeling a little unsure of herself, artistes were again invited to the tea parties which continued, for over 30 years. The Vicar of St.

Andrews Church, Southbourne, has given valuable assistance. Her friend and companion, Miss Meade organised the catering side and became well known among the theatrical profession for her excellent home-made cooking. The afternoon teas started with boiled eggs, two each, if required, cake, shortbread and several cups of tea.

The friendly conversation and meals were enjoyed by all. Spike Milligan, after his first meal, suddenly called out, "I will marry whoever made this cake." Afterwards there was croquet on the lawn. Spike, always the comedian, prostrated himself on the lawn, using his croquet as a billiard cue, to everyone's amusement. If the weather wasn't favourable, there was often an indoor card game.

Originally visitors were asked merely to sign a book with their names and any comments, then photographs were taken on a rather casual basis. Eventually Mrs. Yorke Batley began to realise the importance and usefulness of the photographs. From that time group photos were taken and individual ones were often sent by the artistes. Today she has more than five visitors' books and 25 albums of photographs, To facilitate identification and dates of visits an index card system was developed.

Many hours can be spent delving through these albums. There are youthful photographs of Mike Yarwood, Pete Murray, Max Bygraves, when they were not so well known, a young dark-haired Sean Connery and a charming picture of a laughing Anna Neagle. Cicely Courtneidge came, who had a reputation as a strict disciplinarian to the younger members of her company and insisted on punctual attendance at all the rehearsals. David Nixon was a favourite, also Irene Handl (always with her little dog.)

Hinge and Bracket, those much admired gracious ladies, are regular visitors whenever they are in the area. It is strange to see lovely photographs of them wearing their elegant gowns, and then to see them in another book as two handsome young men. Paul Daniels is another favourite who usually mystifies guests with his amazing dexterity and sleight of hand. Little and Large have been several times. Like Spike Milligan they are entertainers both on and off the stage, particularly the LARGER of the two who brings fun and laughter to any group. Andrew Sachs, (Manuel of Fawlty Towers) is another good friend of Mrs. Yorke Batley and is much more serious than the many amusing roles he plays.

So many famous people have been to the house in Boscombe that it is not possible to mention them all. Roy Castle has been several times, a pleasant and unassuming person both on and off the stage, who was sometimes accompanied by his lovely actress wife. Dulcie Gray sent an attractive close-up of herself as a memento of a happy visit, whilst there are numerous photos of members of the D'Oyly Carte Opera Co., who paid frequent visits to the house for over 25 years.

Many pantomime parties have visited the house, and those in Dick Whittington in 1988/9 were no exception. The large cast included dancers, an Arabian acrobatic troupe, chorus girls and the principal boy. Ruth Madoc and other members of the lively Hi-de-Hi show are always welcome. Former friends who appear at Poole Arts Centre often come to Boscombe to renew their friendship with the two ladies.

I was told an amusing story of Jimmy Edwards who, on receiving his first invitation in the very early days of the tea-parties, firmly declined the invitation. Finally he was persuaded by the doorman at the Pavilion who said, "You should go, you'll enjoy it and he won't preach at you." On his return to the theatre he remarked to the doorman, "You were quite right. I never thought I would enjoy having tea with a b....... parson, and I'll be pleased to see him any time he comes to the theatre".

Another memorable occasion was a visit from the members of the world-famous Bolshoi Ballet, who came one evening. These exceptionally talented dancers were most intrigued with the house and the lovely garden, and through their interpreter, expressed their great pleasure. Sherry was offered to them as to many other guests, but it was obviously not one of their preferred drinks. After they had left, part filled glasses were discovered behind vases and other objects, which made Mrs. Yorke Batley wonder if they would have preferred vodka.

Practically all the artistes who came to Boscombe had been friendly and appreciative, and standards of performance high. There were some changes however. Mrs. Batley remembers young chorus girls who came to the house in the past who were so poorly paid that often the egg meal was their first real one of the day: On Fridays they anxiously waited for their small fee. Child entertainers used to travel with the companies, under strict supervision, and sometimes received tutorial education or attendance at the local school. Today it is simpler and cheaper to use talent from local Dance and Drama Schools. Happily, today, artistes are guaranteed a reasonable salary.

Looking through the Photograph Albums is fascinating – almost a panorama of past and present, as often the same actor and actress appears, and later reappears in other books in different guises and stages of their career.

At certain periods the afternoon teas gave way to morning coffees, with cakes, scones, shortbread, coffee and afterwards sherry, but whether it was morning or afternoon they were always welcome and the two ladies were always thanked for their welcoming invitations.

Today there are fewer shows at the Pavilion, and threats of closure or radical alteration continue to be made to the fine, centrally placed and historical building, erected in 1929. But former friends performing at the Poole Arts Centre Theatre often visited Boscombe to renew their friendship with the two ladies.

The happy parties continued until 1989 when due to health problems they had regretfully to be ceased.

An unexpected and surprising event also occurred in 1989 and one much appreciated by Mrs. Yorke Batley an invitation to the BBC studios in London, to appear, with her companion, Miss Meade, in the Esther Ranzten programme – HEARTS OF GOLD.

Like many of these programmes, the event was carried out in secret and Mrs. Yorke Batley was only informed that a documentary was in process of being made on provincial theatres and her views were requested for the programme. There was great excitement when Esther Rantzen and her team of assistants and camera men came to the house in Boscombe and spent a whole day filming there – but there was still no mention of the HEARTS OF GOLD programme. When the two ladies arrived at the studio, they only discovered, to their amazement, and when they were actually on the stage, that they were an important part of this programme.

It was a wonderful evening. Mrs. Yorke Batley was greeted by Leslie Crowther who was responsible for persuading her to continue the theatrical parties after her husband's death in 1960. Then Hinge and Bracket arrived, gloriously attired in magnificent Victorian gowns and greeted the two ladies, followed by Bracket singing 'Dreaming of a White Christmas' as snowflakes gently fluttered down. There was more excitement again when Ruth Madoc, Little and Large, Spike Milligan, Russ Abbot and Paul Daniels appeared in turn on a huge screen, and each gave appreciative words of greeting. Both ladies were presented with HEARTS OF GOLD badges by Leslie Crowther which they prize very much.

Taken home in a limousine, they arrived in Bournemouth after midnight and after a memorable day they will never forget. But there was a further surprise in store for the 'party-lady' when in December, 1989, she was awarded a BRITISH EMPIRE MEDAL in the Queen's New Year Honours List for her services to the theatrical profession in Bournemouth.

Mrs. Yorke Batley, who looks so much more youthful than her turned 90 years, has decided, eventually, to bequeath her wonderful collection to the Victoria and Albert Museum when her unique collection will be seen by a wider audience and the wonderful and enjoyable work undertaken by the two ladies will live forever.

KAREN LONDON
CABARET ARTISTE

–and–

ANIMAL TRAINER

Show business has lured Karen London away from Bournemouth, but she has vowed to return to the seaside resort that has brought her so much happiness. The life of that amazing, talented lady has been surrounded by cabaret dancing and animals, particularly dogs – oh! and being a Lady Clown.

From earliest childhood Karen had loved dogs, admiring that much-loved film dog, Lassie, and showing their family Border Terrier how to do simple tricks. When she was about 10 years old she was given her own puppy, a Border Terrier called Bambi which had been rescued by her grandmother from destruction. Karen had soon taught a willing Bambi to do most of the tricks of Lassie.

Her first choice of a career was as a Veterinary Surgeon, but the training cost too much money, "and I was lacking in little grey cells" grimaced Karen so she turned to her second choice – dancing. She had been to dancing classes from childhood. Without difficulty Karen became a cabaret artiste with engagements in this country and abroad. In India the King of Nepal proposed marriage to the attractive dancer, but Karen wanted to return home.

Her move to Bournemouth in the 60's marked a change in her life. There were many singing and dancing engagements at the top Bournemouth hotels, but her love and attachment for dogs remained as strong as ever.

When a friend of hers rescued a poor, little, shivering puppy, which had been left in the snow – an unwanted Christmas present – Karen was asked to care for the wet and bedraggled bundle of misery. Karen's heart went out to the little puppy. She named him Benjie, and after a few days of warmth and comfort he became a lively little puppy. But Benjie was no ordinary puppy and Karen soon realised that he was highly intelligent. In fact soon she was referring to Benjie as a 'genius'.

To Karen's amazement, the tiny puppy, so grateful for his new home and his loving mistress, began to do tricks on his own, fetching and carrying objects, even jumping, rolling over and begging. Karen had to think of new ideas to show him. It was as though the little dog was saying 'Please show me some more tricks; I enjoy doing them' At a few months old he was doing the exercises of top obedience dogs.

Benjie's first acting début was at Bournemouth Aqua Circus. Karen had been engaged as Ring Mistress for the season and Benjie was welcomed as an additional part of the show. But Benjie was fearful of other people, and cringed away from children who merely wanted to stroke him. To accustom him to others, Karen decided to leave him with a friend and her family. But Karen became worried when she say the pleading look on his face as though to say 'Please don't leave me here.' Wondering if she had done the right thing, Karen returned home.

When she reached her door, she could hardly believe it. There sat Benjie, wagging his tail. He had slipped away from her friend's house, and although they had journeyed by car, he had actually found his way back on foot, crossing several busy main roads. As Karen hugged the little animal, she vowed she would never leave him again.

Karen was delighted when she received her first television engagement – to appear on Multi Coloured Swap Shop in the company of Noel Edmonds and Barbara Woodhouse. Benjie was then one year old and some of the tricks they had practised, especially for the Show, were quite new ones, but the show was a great success. Benjie's 'pièce de résistance' was when he was blindfolded, jumped through a hoop of solid paper, picked up a flag, which read 'Bye–Bye', returned through the hoop and gave the flag to Karen. Benjie's fame was spreading and soon there were other engagements. There were bookings from holiday camps, summer gâlas and children's entertainments, when Benjie was billed as BENJIE WONDER DOG, THE LITTLE DOG WITH THE BIG I.Q. To add to the entertainment Karen became a lady clown with curly red hair – 'the only professional woman clown in Britain at that time.' said Karen. Benjie became well known on local radio, barking the correct answers to phone-in questions. He appeared in Super Store, with Mike Reid, the D.J. and also followed the penguins on two legs in the Penguin Biscuit advertisement, but besides all this he was a real friend to his mistress, carrying objects for her, picking up the phone and really looking after her. "There will never be another dog like Benjie" said Karen. "He is a wonder dog and quite unique". Sadly Benjie died suddenly at the age of 9 years, after being bitten on the back by another dog. Karen was heart-broken. Through her other dogs, their love and affection, and the continuation of their training programmes, Karen slowly regained her composure. There was Collie-wobbles, who took over from Benjie. At first he was too enthusiastic, even doing the trick before he had received the command to the delight of the audience. After a season in Devon, Colly Wobbles became a crowd puller. He appeared in 'It's Wicked' from Torquay for Granada and with all the stars from HI-DE-HI, Michael Barrymore and many more.

A move to the Midlands seemed a good idea due to its central position to the rest of Britain.

TVS was the first Television Company to engage them from there. Wobbles became the mind-reading dog with Chris Tarrant on PROVE IT, followed by a children's programme called MOTOR MOUTH. He is also part of a six-dog team that entertains at Fetes and Garden Parties. Collie Flower, a young relation to Colly Wobbles has now become the children's entertainer at children's parties, as 'Wobbie' is 10 now.

Collie Flower gave birth to the NEW BEN, named in Benjie's honour and is proving to be as good as the original BEN. "To me, he is very special" said Karen, "almost as if he were my old Ben reincarnated." The new Ben won his first Obedience Show in Bournemouth in 1991 and was selected out of hundreds of dogs to be the Crown Berger dog in the 1992 commercial. Karen feels that one day he will get to Crufts as OBEDIENCE CHAMPION. Ben's father is TROY, the dog who rides a bike on the Rowan Atkinson show on TV; also TROY was the first animal to ever perform at the Royal Albert Hall on January 1st 1992. Karen says how proud she is of her family of dogs. "They are all family and friends, and first and foremost they are respected and given the freedom of any ordinary dog." Their versatility is only equalled by their clever mistress, all her acts being accomplished by love, caring and fun – and the move back to Bournemouth is still on the calendar!

EDNA DAWES – THE LUCKY E.D'S

Bournemouth is fortunate in having a world famous, international lady writer in its midst, who, already, has written over 15 novels, published in hardback, paperback, large print, and translated into many languages. Her name is Edna Dawes, but not always. Sometimes it is Elizabeth Darrell or Emma Drummond, or even Eva Dane or Eleanor Drew. Five well known names and they all belong to the same person.

When Edna started writing in 1976 she discovered that her writing ability and speed were too much for one publisher, so the other E.D's came into existence – 'her lucky initials!' With each name comes a different type of writing, romantic for Eva Dane and Eleanor Drew; historical and military army for Emma Drummond and family sagas and military aviation for Elizabeth Darrell. Publishers are happy and so is this prolific writer.

Born in Essex in a large military family – her father and four uncles served in the Royal Engineers – Edna spent most of her early childhood in Hongkong. On leaving grammar school, she became a draughtswoman and then joined the WRAC, becoming a Training Officer and travelling around Europe on her leave.

When she married Ken, a scientific officer with the Ministry of Defence in Portsmouth, his work soon took them to many more exotic places, including three years in Singapore.

Not surprisingly her well researched books reveal her exciting life in many different countries – and not surprisingly, her first novel, a romantic thriller, was situated in Singapore and written under her own name.

How did all this come about? As a young school girl her burning ambition was to achieve fame as a Wimbledon champion or to become a world famous opera singer, or, lastly a well known writer.

Although she gained several cups for tennis playing, she felt she had not the dedication or temperament to continue. Laughingly she remarked, "I could have ended up as a frustrated female McInroe." Singing moderately well with theatre groups, it was nevertheless, her last choice which became the important one.

So how did she achieve success with her Number 3 choice without influential connections in the publishing world or any other advantage save talent and massive determination? She wrote a romantic thriller and immediately embarked on another while the first was going the rounds of publishers. Family commitments had delayed her ambition for so long that she was loath to waste time, while rejection slips piled up.

But after only ten months her first novel, 'Dearest Tiger' under the name of EDNA DAWES had been accepted and was in the shops. The second swiftly followed . . . and the third. Beginning as a writer of contemporary romance and adventures, her interest in military history, her background of the army and navy and experience of life overseas, soon became an important part of her writing. As the words poured from her, plots became even more dramatic and gripping, while new ideas of love, hate, life and death poured from her vivid imagination.

The new names became a necessity. "My dear husband sometimes wonders who he is really married to," Edna claims with a smile.

From Portsmouth they moved to Bournemouth. "Why Bournemouth?" I queried. "As a writer you can live almost anywhere" said Edna. "All areas provide scope for realistic background and true descriptions of the surrounding countryside. Many happy holidays had been spent in Bournemouth when the children were younger and they had never forgotten the delights of sea bathing, the golden sands, wandering in the New Forest and the wonderful Dorset scenery with quaint thatched cottages".

Although the complex plots and varying characters, the introverted, the extroverted, the kind and the cruel, are figments of her own brain, research is thorough, taking Edna to many more interesting places. For a book on the Boer War, she visited the actual hotel in Ladysmith where the first shell had landed. On a visit to Kruger Park with its large game reserve, she spent exciting days watching and studying the habits of wild animals. A trilogy of modern adventure thrillers in South Africa proved a great success.

As diamonds were a sparkling feature of the books, she visited the mine where the famous Cullinan stone had been found. No one is allowed to descend the mine, and only permitted to visit the surface buildings, accompanied by a guide. Security is strict and everyone is examined to ensure that no hidden diamonds are secreted on their person. If anything is dropped only the guide is allowed to pick it up.

Visitors, however, are allowed to go down gold mines which Edna found uncomfortably claustrophobic. She remembers the terrifying speed of the cage as it rushed down, over 4,000 feet into the bowels of the earth and right down to the drilling surface "when you feel the noise could break your ear drums". Again there is strict security, although visitors are told they may take one of the golden bars if they can lift it. No one ever can!

Edna even rode an ostrich when researching into ostrich farms, and after three men had fallen off. There was a visit to an opium den in Singapore to research an authentic background for an early novel about the disappearance of a Chinese girl. Edna shudders as she recalled the dark, dimly lit room, smelling of sickly incense and the thin, emaciated, weak addicts, squatting on the dirty floor, kept alive by their drugs but with an unpleasant death facing them.

As the number of books increased, Edna's husband resigned from the Ministry of Defence to become Edna's manager and partner, helping to research important details, particularly military data.

Obtaining atmosphere for a book based on her father's army experiences in North Russia in 1919, proved difficult. Her husband, then still working for the Ministry of Defence, had to get clearance from the department to go behind the Iron Curtain, but his mother became ill and the visit was cancelled. They did, however, manage a visit to Czechoslovakia, but his passport identified him as an employee of the Ministry of Defence, and approaches were actually made in an effort to lure them both into an illegal financial transaction. They had been warned that the Czech regime of that time might try a variety of tricks in an attempt to discredit him and withhold his passport. Edna, who usually saw the amusing side of their adventures, remarked "I was hoping he was going to be offered seduction by an attractive Olga so that I could write a book about it, but there was nothing romantic about this affair and we were both relieved when the Iron Curtain was behind us with us on the other side of it."

Shortly after moving to Dorset and to show her attachment to the county, she wrote a book on the Tarrants in Dorset – AT THE GOING DOWN OF THE SUN. In it, Edna created some more Tarrants – Tarrant Royal, Tarrant Maundle, Greater Tarrant but throughout there is the real village atmosphere of the real Tarrants showing the village community life during the period of the First World War. The story is gripping and at times, traumatic, revealing the horrors of the war period which sadly affected the lives of three brothers who had inherited Tarrant Hall and whose roots were in the village life with its cricket matches on the green, and colourful summer fêtes. Everywhere you can almost see the picturesque, thatched cottages, often with climbing roses alongside the wall. There are ancient churches with square, stone towers, lush, green rolling hills, the old village pond and wild flowers everywhere. The effects of the war on the brothers was devastating and often sad. The book was a great success, while many members of the public and Edna feel that what happened to the characters affected the lives of many likeable young men of that period. The Americans, with their love of history and ancient buildings, bought more and more copies of this fascinating novel. The sequel AND IN THE MORNING continued the story in the 1939–45 war, while the Americans continue to be enthralled with Dorset village life and quaint Dorset characters.

IN THE FLIGHT OF THE FLAMINGO by Elizabeth Darrell, the study of flying boats came well to the fore. Edna had found the theme fascinating enough to demand a novel on those glamorous, charismatic aircraft. To get the real feel of flying boats Edna visited the Hall of Aviation in Southampton where she was allowed to sit at the controls of an old Empire Flying Boat. Hearing of a reunion of members of a flying boat association, she contacted the chairman who lived in Christchurch, and through him met an ex-flying captain and learnt more again about this thrilling way of life. It was decided at this stage that military army books should be left to EMMA DRUMMOND and military aviation to ELIZABETH DARRELL. These now so fully occupied this husband and wife partnership that the romantic thrillers, and with them, EVA DANE and ELEANOR DREW had to be abandoned.

Fierce battles were sometimes fought with her publishers as Edna persevered and pressed her case for recognitions as an authoritative female military writer. While not a feminist, Edna realised that victories could be obtained from a feminine attitude, bringing in thankfulness for the acceptance of her views.

Edna usually manages to write two books each year. As the plots and stories become more dramatic, involved, and lives more complicated, their length has increased, often to over 600 pages, which means that the two a year aim has become more difficult.

This amazing lady sees the plot of her novels unfold before her very eyes almost as if they were real people acting a saga in front of her. Her characters are REAL people to her, and as she is writing she suffers their heart aches and rejoices in their triumphs. When each novel ends she knows a deep sense of sadness at parting with characters she has grown to care for in the same way her legion of readers do. Publishers often believe in a happy ending, despite the many traumas of love and war. Edna finds that is not always possible, but usually she predicts hope ahead at the last chapter.

Her books are a huge favourite in libraries, and were recently listed in the top 27. They are read equally by men and women, while readers write from all parts of the world with stories of ancestors who took part in campaigns in 'Drummond' books and with recollections of being stationed in the Tarrants after reading 'Darrell.'

Almost unbelievable, in these days of technical achievement, word processors, and computers this up-to-date, well-travelled lady writes all her drafts in long-hand. Go into her sprawling study in her house by the sea and you see pile upon pile of hand written manuscripts – which are afterwards typed on her electric typewriter.

Edna Dawes, five authors in one, your stories of war, endeavour and family loyalty, with love triumphing over all, will live for many years to come, and continue to give pleasure to your present day army of world wide readers.

BIBLIOGRAPHY

Battrick, Jack- as told by Gail Lawson. Brownsea Island, 1978.

Boodle, Adelaide A. R.L.S. and his SINE QUA NON – Flashlights from Skerry-more – by the Gamekeeper 1926.

Bruce, George. A Family and a Fortune, Bournemouth and the Cooper Deans. 1987.

Colvin, Sidney. Robert Louis Stevenson. Letters to his Family and Friends, Vol. I and II – Selected and edited with Notes and Introductions by, 1899.

Edwards, Elizabeth. A History of Bournemouth, 1981.

Gittings, Robert. The Older Hardy, 1978.

Grylls, R. Glynn, Mary Shelley. A Biography. 1938.

Hammerton, J.A. Stevensoniana, An anecdotal life and appreciation of Robert Louis Stevenson. 1907.

Hardy, Thomas. Festival Official Handbook, July 7th – 20th. 1968.

Hatts, Leigh. The Fabians in Bournemouth. 1984.

Havers QC. The Right Hon Sir Michael, Shankland, Peter, and Barrett, Anthony. The Rattenbury Murders. 1980.

Kay-Robinson, Denys. The First Mrs. Thomas Hardy. 1979.

Mate, Charles H. and Riddle, Charles. Bournemouth. 1810–1910. 1910.

Muggeridge, Kitty and Adams, Ruth. Beatrice Webb – A Life – 1858–1943. 1967.

Norman, Sylva. Flight of the Skylark – The Development of Shelley's Reputation. 1954.

Russell-Cotes, Sir, J.P. Home and Abroad – An Autobiography of an Octogenarian Vols I and II. 1921.

The Sheldon Press. Brave Dame Mary or The Seige of Corfe Castle. 1873.

Short, Bernard C. A Short History of Brownsea Island. 1972.

Steuart J.A. Robert Louis Stevenson. Man & Writer. 1924.

Stewart, J.L.M. Thomas Hardy. 1971.

Sutton, Jean, and Bromby, Alan. Brownsea Island – A History.

Ward, Ted, Dr. The Guests of Canford Manor. 1992.

Young, David S. The Story of Bournemouth. 1957.

Other titles available from
POWER PUBLICATIONS

Pub Walks series
PUB WALKS IN DORSET
FORTY MORE PUB WALKS IN DORSET
PUB WALKS IN HAMPSHIRE AND I.O.W.
PUB WALKS IN WEST SUSSEX
PUB WALKS IN DEVON.   spring 93
PUB WALKS IN CORNWALL.   spring 93

Other local interest books